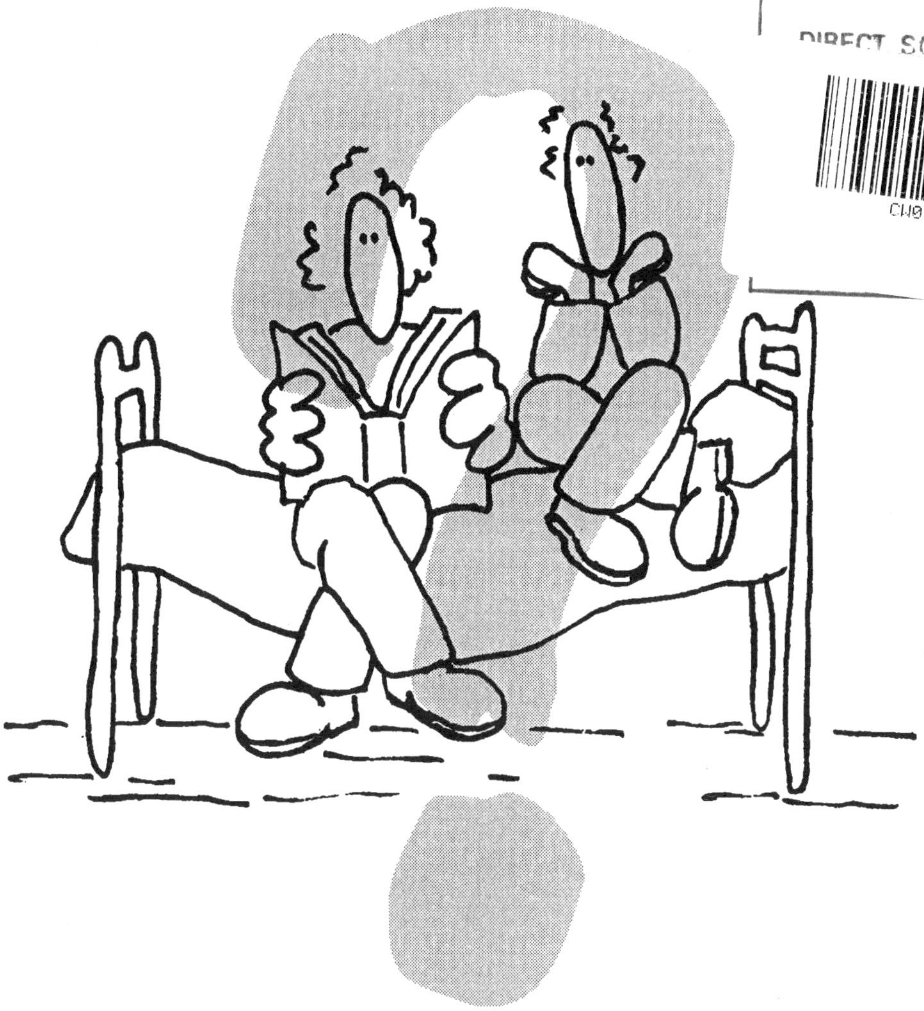

ANSWERS

A Handbook for Residential and Foster Carers of young people aged 11-18 years

by Ann Wheal

in collaboration with Ann Buchanan

Published by
Longman Information and Reference,
Longman Group UK Ltd, 6th Floor, Westgate House, The High, Harlow,
Essex, CM20 1YR, England and Associated Companies throughout the world.

© Longman Group UK Ltd 1994

All rights reserved. No part of this publication may be reproduced, stored in a retrieval system, or transmitted in any form or by any means, electronic, mechanical, photocopying, recording or otherwise, without the prior permission of the Copyright Licensing Agency Ltd., 90 Tottenham Court Road, London W1P 9HE.

Photocopying Permission: Permission is granted by the copyright holders/publisher for photocopying this material within institutions purchasing the material.

A catalogue record for this book is available from The British Library

ISBN 0-582-24468-4

Typeset by
Ashford Open Learning, 1 Church Road, Shedfield, Hampshire, SO3 2HW
Telephone: 0329 833111

Printed by Page Bros, Norwich

ANSWERS – CONTENTS

INTRODUCTION

	Page
Foreword	iv
Background	vi
Inch by Inch – Setting up Young People to Succeed	1
How the Book Works	2
Carer's Responsibilities	4
Training Support and Guidance for Carers	6
Who's Who in Helping Young People	8

BEING LOOKED AFTER

Being Looked After	10
Meetings	11
Planning Meetings	15
Reviews	17
Child Protection Conference/Register	19
Working with Parents	21
Collecting Mementos	24
Life Story Work	25
Complaints	26
Discrimination	28

PLACES TO LIVE

Places to Live: Foster Homes	32
Children's Homes	33
Secure Units	34
The Home Environment	35

PRACTICAL INFORMATION

Money	37
Managing Money/Budgeting/Saving	39
Managing Money Checklist	41
Education	43
Education – A Young Person's Checklist	45
Qualifications	48
Leisure – What to do in Free Time	51
Health	54
Health Record Sheet	61
Drug Abuse	63
Solvent Abuse	67
HIV/Aids	70
Personal Relationships and Sex	71
Staying with Friends	75
Part Time Jobs	76

EMOTIONAL/SOCIAL INFORMATION

Growing Up	78
Decision Making	79
Encouraging Positive Behaviour	83
Privacy/Confidentiality	87
Self Respect/Self Esteem/Confidence	88
Know Yourself – Checklist	89
Values	91
Listening and Being Listened to	92
Making and Keeping Friends	94
Coping with Crisis	96
Worries	98
Worries – Checklist	101
Identifying Abuse	103
Bullying	107
Loss & Bereavement	108

BECOMING INDEPENDENT

A Young Person's View	110
Preparation and Planning	111
Housing	114
Housing Checklist	116
Getting a Job – A Young Person's Checklist	117
Careers	126
Work	127
Feeling Isolated and Lonely – Support Networks	130
Becoming Independent	132
Independence Checklist	133

LEGAL

Court Orders and the Children Act	141
Being Accommodated	142
Court Orders – An Outline Summary of What they Mean	143
Independent Visitor	148
Adoption	151
Guardian Ad Litem	153
Guardianship	154
Wardship and the Inherent Jurisdiction	155
Youth Justice	156
Records	158
Parental Responsibility	162
Changing Names	163

OTHER INFORMATION

Suggestions Sheet	165
Useful Telephone Numbers & Addresses	167
Acknowledgements	174
Sources of Reference	175
Index	178

FOREWORD

During 1992 Ann Wheal and Ann Buchanan from the University of Southampton, came to see me to talk about the Dolphin Project. One of the principle findings from this research was that many carers were worried about telling young people about their rights and responsibilities, and many young people had insufficient information to make the necessary decisions in their lives. I realized that if we could find a small sum of money towards to the costs of a publication that would give carers and young people in England and Wales the information they needed in an accessible form, this would be a worthwhile contribution by CCETSW. In 1993, this became possible.

Work on ANSWERS has proceeded with remarkable speed. Drafts of the handbook have been piloted, critically read and evaluated. The comments of the carers and the young people who have tried it out have been taken very seriously. There have been occasions when their opinions as to what was needed have, quite rightly, overridden our own views.

The result is a handbook covering a very wide range of topics written with as little jargon as possible, yet firmly rooted within the relevant legislation.

The handbook provides a potential resource for a large number of carers, young people and students. It can reduce the isolation of foster carers who often have the task of answering difficult questions without the information they need, and without colleagues at hand, in their time of need.

I hope that at least one copy will find its way to every children's home where it will be discussed by staff prior to its being used. It has potential for integration into agency-based training, and the University of Southampton has plans for the production of associated training materials.

At the time of writing, NVQ standards specifically for work with young people are not yet available. These are now being developed and should be published together with awards at different levels during 1995. Meanwhile there are relevant standards elsewhere that can be used with appropriate advice from those knowledgeable about NVQ. These are found for example in the standards relating to Criminal Justice and the Care Awards.

In relation to the Diploma in Social Work, CCETSW is closely involved in the promotion and development of residential child care. This is happening on eight programmes in England which are receiving special funding, but other programmes are also involved and there is now a keen interest in providing high standards of training as part of professional qualifications. The handbook is likely to be particularly helpful in the preparation of students who have not had a background in residential child care before enrolling on a DipSW course and who undertake practice placements in children's homes.

Finally I would like all those who use this handbook, whether directly at work or in training, to do so within the context of the views expressed in Setting Quality Standards for Residential Child Care: A Practical Way Forward (CCETSW 1992). The writers' group expressed that "any attempt to itemize the rights and needs of children risks reducing their humanity: it is only through commitment and engagement with each child, through their development over time, that the complexity and individuality of their rights and needs can be addressed. Children in the public care share needs with all children, yet their particular experiences bring additional vulnerabilities; their status in the care system can be a further source of oppression. Training in residential child care must attempt to equip students to relate to the whole child, experience, history, feelings, strengths, dependence, day-to-day habits, aspirations. All these will affect how any child may respond to the daily regime. Staff will be unlikely to offer effective help to children who are powerless if they themselves are part of the system which devalues them".

Ultimately it is whether we succeed in making young people in residential and foster care feel more valued and powerful that will be the true test of ANSWERS.

Clare Roskill
Programme Head, Child Care
CCETSW Central Office February 1994

FOREWORD

We welcome the publication of this handbook which will no doubt help to fill a huge and worrying gap in the available material. Young people and their carers have long needed an informative, accessible, and easy to use handbook which would provide vital information about their rights and responsibilities. This handbook addresses this need, and as such, lays the foundation for further development in a much-needed but neglected area of work.

Christine Hammond
Director
BAAF (British Agencies for Adoption and Fosterers)

A very good handbook for new foster carers. Full of useful information and easy to understand. The best yet *(Foster carer. Derby)*.

I was particularly impressed that there is a distinct lack of jargon. It certainly made the introduction of our latest foster child very easy. *(Foster carer. Derby)*.

Use of the handbook was very good as a back up to what I had already explained to the client. I could then show the client and they could read it easily to confirm my decision. Open discussions amongst the children are great. They can air their grievances etc. which can help a sometimes explosive situation. Involving the clients builds up interest, self-esteem etc. Very good. *(Care assistant. Brecon)*.

Extremely useful for in-house training for staff, residents, foster carers and clients; supervision with staff and residents; staff meetings and residents meetings; a quick reference for service users, families and friends. Available for residents, families, friends and community *(Residential carer. Ladywood, Birmingham)*.

I found this handbook excellent. The most informative information I've ever received, both for myself and the young people I care for. *(Foster carer. Mid-Wales)*.

Very useful for NVQ and social care related courses. Dip SW students and experienced residential workers should be familiar with most of the contents. Direct entry students and students on placement would also find it especially useful, also casual and new staff. *(Residential manager. Hampshire)*.

When I came into residential work, I had little or no induction or training and learnt as I went along. A book such as this would have been invaluable to me. A book like this could ensure that all staff have some training whatever the level they are employed at. *(RSSO student. Hampshire)*.

BACKGROUND

In 1992 the Department of Social Work Studies at the University of Southampton took part in a research project which became known as the DOLPHIN PROJECT.

During the project, Ann Wheal and Daphne Walder met young people who were being looked after in Birmingham, Berkshire and Hampshire. They told us what they knew about the Children Act and also about their time in children's homes and in foster care. Ann Buchanan also met their carers.

A report, called 'Answering Back' – A young person's view of the Children Act has now been published. It is available from Department of Social Work Studies, University of Southampton, Southampton, SO9 5NH.

ANSWERS is one of the many outcomes of this report.

This book will seek to ensure that there is no unfair discrimination on the grounds of age, gender, disability (including use of sign language), race, ethnic origin, nationality, sexual orientation, social class, religion or language.

INCH BY INCH – SETTING UP YOUNG PEOPLE TO SUCCEED

This book is about Rights and Responsibilities. What exactly do we mean? Whose Rights? Whose Responsibilities? The Young Person's or the Carer's? The answer is "Both".

By using this book as a guide we hope you will work with the young people in your care, explaining to them:

- exactly what their rights are

- how important it is to use these rights

- how to use these rights responsibly

The more information young people have the better equipped they will be to make decisions that affect their lives. This doesn't happen overnight. They need to be taught skills to help them make these decisions and when these decisions turn out to be wrong, how to pick up the pieces and start again, no matter how painful.

There is an old saying "He who has never made a mistake, has never made anything". This is true of us all and the young people in your care need your time and patience as well as all the information you can give them to help them make informed choices and sensible decisions about their lives.

Some people may think that if a young person is given too much information it may be abused. Our experience points to the reverse. The more information young people have the better able they are to successfully plan their lives and their future.

Everyone needs to be valued, to feel special, to feel important. Sometimes the backgrounds and experiences of black or other ethnic minority young people are undervalued. By treating all young people as individuals, working with and caring for them, you will build up their self esteem.

HOW THE BOOK WORKS

This handbook has been produced for residential and foster carers in England and Wales.

The Children Act which came into effect in 1991 was designed to:

- encourage carers to work in partnership with young people in their care

- encourage young people to return to their parent(s)' home as soon as possible if appropriate

- encourage those looking after the young people to work with them in all sorts of ways, so that these young people will be able to take their place in society in the future

This book has been developed:

- for young people and carers to read together

- to help carers answer the many questions a young person aged 11-18 may ask about the Children Act

- to help carers answer the many questions a young person aged 11-18 may ask about their time being looked after

- to be used as a 'talking tool' when carers are working in partnership with young people, either in groups or one-to-one. In this way it is hoped young people will learn to take responsibility for their own future

The book contains many topics that may be used as a way to start talking with young people about issues that extend beyond the home. Some of the sheets contain questions a young person might ask. These are shown in circles. We have then given some suggested answers.

We have included checklists and extra information that will only be of interest to particular young people at particular times. These have been written as though they are for the young person.

The checklist and forms may be photocopied without permission

Where other organisations are mentioned the address and/or telephone number can be found at the back of the book.

No mention has been made of benefit entitlement as these vary with individual circumstances. They are included in "Stepping Out" mentioned on page 113.

Guidance and Regulations have been produced by the Department of Health explaining the meaning of the Children Act. We have shown at the foot of the page throughout the book, the appropriate Guidance and Regulations volumes and page numbers. Children's homes and social services area offices should have copies available for reference.

This handbook has been written so that it may also be useful for those being assessed for NVQ qualifications and for those undertaking residential child care placements while studying for the Diploma in Social Work.

It is hoped shortly to produce training/self-assessment materials to be used in conjunction with this handbook.

> "A good carer is someone who sits down and listens to you and discusses things with you"
>
> young person's view

CARER'S RESPONSIBILITIES

Our research suggests the following are the responsibilities of a carer.

A carer should be able to:

- provide each young person with food, clothing, a bed and a small personal area, or separate room if possible

- include each young person in the activities of the home

- establish clear expectations and limits

- discipline fairly

- deal with negative behaviour in a positive way

- reward good behaviour

- promote and encourage a relationship with birth family

- encourage a young person's cultural and religious heritage and behave in a way which does not discriminate

- arrange for routine and emergency medical and dental care

- assume responsibility for the young person's daily school activities

- ensure that the young person's educational needs are met

- promote a young person's self-esteem and positive self-image

- respect the young person and his/her birth family

- work with all concerned, including the young person, to make a permanent plan for them

- help prepare the young person to return to his/her birth family or be placed with relatives or friends, adoptive parent(s), or to live independently

- help the young person to speak up, to be heard and to be listened to

- to listen, to understand and to relate to each young person

> There may be others you think should be added to this list?

The following are some things the young people who took part in the Dolphin Project wanted from their carers. They wanted them to:

- share information with the young person about his or her rights under the law and make sure that the young person fully understands any legal order affecting him/her

- acknowledge difference whether due to racial origin, language, religion or culture; respect and support young people and challenge discrimination

- provide opportunities for young people to make choices and to learn about making decisions; involve them in planning

- remember that in dealing with parent(s), young people are also partners in the decision-making and may need support in making their views known

- help young people to participate in their reviews

- prepare young people for independence

- share information about pocket money and allowances

- support young people in making a complaint

- help young people develop other relationships, other partnerships

- advocate for young people in obtaining equal opportunity in education

- recognise and support young people in distress

- **recognise that the best partner may be the key residential worker or foster carer**

(Buchanan, A, 1993)

TRAINING SUPPORT AND GUIDANCE FOR CARERS

The aim of CCETSW – The Central Council for Education and Training in Social Work – is to:

- promote quality education and training in social work

- award qualifications in social work

- work closely with other organisations to develop training and training materials suitable for all areas of care

CCETSW funded the pilot stage of this handbook as part of its commitment to quality care and training.

1   National Vocational Qualifications (NVQ)

These are work-based qualifications where the skills and tasks carers do in their work are assessed whilst at work. Carers and the assessor, usually a colleague, negotiate what evidence of a particular task is needed and how and when it will be gathered.

The assessor records the evidence which is then included in the portfolio of the carer. When there is evidence of competence in sufficient units the carer will be awarded the relevant NVQ.

There is no time limit to these awards. Many people take about two years but it can take a shorter time depending on experience and on the assessment arrangements. Work done in the past may also count towards the award. A unit cannot be failed. If the carer is found 'not yet competent' they can get more help and try again.

At present there are three sets of awards each of which is offered at more than one level. There is a major project which has been funded to develop standards specifically for those working with children and young people aged 8-18 years in a range of settings.

Awards based on these standards are likely to become available in 1995 or 1996. Meanwhile if you wish to start gathering evidence of competence using the units that exist already, contact:

NCVQ, 222 EUSTON ROAD, LONDON NW1 2BZ or

CCETSW, DERBYSHIRE HOUSE, ST CHAD'S STREET, LONDON WC1H 8AD

Note: some colleges are also offering courses linked to NVQ

2 Diploma in Social Work

This award is the professional qualification for all areas of social work, including work with children and young people.

If your employer agrees, you may be able to apply for an employment based route and continue to be employed and paid a salary whilst being trained.

Students attend college either full time or part time. Most programmes last two years. The content of the programme is designed to meet the various needs of the students who may have very different backgrounds and experience. In the second year carers can concentrate on work with children and families or on other areas.

It is proposed that open and distance learning arrangements will be available shortly.

For more details contact CCETSW at the above address or a local college with a Dip SW programme.

3 Postqualifying and Advanced Awards in Social Work

These are two new awards for those who already have a Diploma in Social Work. They are becoming available in stages across the UK and should be available in most areas by 1995.

Credits are gained towards the awards through work being assessed and approved. This can be done over a period of time. Work done in the past can also count towards these awards.

For more details contact CCETSW at the above address.

4 Other Training Courses

There are also many training courses available on subjects such as:

Counselling • Drug Abuse • Family Assistance •

HIV/Aids • Disability • Children Act

You may be asked to attend or you could ask to attend. It's a good idea to read up about the course before you attend and to share with others what you have learned when you return.

Ref. No: G&R V4 p7-9 V3 p31-32

WHO'S WHO IN HELPING YOUNG PEOPLE

The best helpers are often the young person's family and friends. But the following may also be involved:

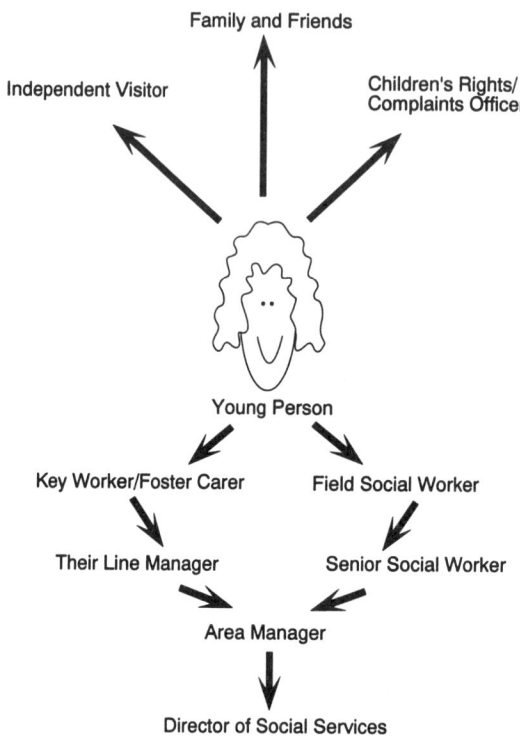

Key worker
In residential settings the keyworkers are responsible for the young people. They build a relationship with the young person, assess the young person's needs, and help to meet those needs. They are involved with admissions; planning; liaising with other agencies and with parent(s); for the overall well being of the young person.

Foster carer (sometimes known as family based carer)
Foster carers have an agreement with a social service. The young person lives in the foster carer's own home. There are many different types of foster carers: short term, long term and specialist foster carers who are trained and have chosen to look after teenagers, young people with disabilities or those with behavioural problems. Foster carers also like to get to know a young person really well and help them in many different ways.

Field social worker
All young people who are being looked after should have a field social worker who is based in the local area office from which the young person came. In some areas they are called care managers. Generally speaking their job is to keep in touch with the young person, their family and residential or foster carers, and to make sure plans are carried out. They usually attend planning meetings and reviews, and handle any court matters. The field social worker is the first line of contact for the young person and the residential and foster carer.

Key worker's line manager
This is the person who is responsible for the key worker. Key workers will go to their line manager for advice and guidance. This person may be the manager of the home. If a young person has a disagreement with their key worker, they may want to discuss this with another worker or the line manager.

Family placement worker/Foster carer's social worker
Most foster carers will have their own social worker who is based in the Fostering Family Placement office. This person advises the foster carer about general fostering issues. They are similar to the key worker's line manager.

Team managers/Area managers/Directors of social services
Most social service departments are organised like pyramids, with team managers, area managers and deputy directors and finally the director. Each level is responsible for the level below. It is a good idea to find out how your social services are organised as occasionally you might need the help of someone very senior.

Children's rights officer
Many areas now have such a person who is usually separate from social workers. Young people in residential and foster care should be able to telephone the CRO and discuss in confidence anything that is bothering them.

Independent visitor
Young people who are not in touch with their families may have an independent visitor. See page 148.

OTHER HELPERS WHO MAY BE INVOLVED

Education welfare officers
Their job is to be a link between the school and the residential or foster home. They talk to the school about any problem a young person may be having at school, for example, bullying. They are also involved when a young person is truanting. They can usually be contacted through the school.

Educational psychologist
If a young person is having real difficulties in learning or concentrating at school, the head teacher may ask for a an educational psychologist to see him/her. An educational psychologist is not a psychiatrist, but someone who has special knowledge about how children learn and what may be causing them to have difficulties. Educational psychologists are involved when young people need specific educational help to overcome their difficulties.

Child guidance workers
Child guidance workers help young people who may have an emotional or behavioural problem in particular because of some earlier unhappy experience. A child psychiatrist will be part of the team which includes psychologists and specialist social workers. With the help of the young person, their carer and/or their family, the child guidance worker draws up a plan to overcome the difficulties.

BEING LOOKED AFTER

When a young person is first looked after by social services the young person will probably have been under considerable strain and stress so it is very important that this early stage is well planned and handled carefully.

Each young person will be different and will need to be treated differently:

- they may want to be on their own   or
- to talk to you alone   or
- to talk to another young person   or
- to very quickly become one of the 'gang'

Quite often they may be rude or aggressive or even totally silent and not eat. Whatever their reaction in the first few days let them be alone – yet not alone – 'be alert, watch and observe and be there when needed'.

Gradually try to persuade them to take part in the life of their new home. Give them a welcoming, warm environment. Explain what is going on, why they are there, and if you know, how long for.

Tell them how the system works, who is responsible for them and who they can go to if they need help.

Let them tell you about their previous experience, where they lived and what the rules were.

They could make a list, with addresses if possible, in case they need the information later. They could also list their previous schools and the names and addresses of people who are important to them.

If they don't know:

- explain what a social worker does
- what their court order means if they have one
- what the many new terms they will hear mean

It will all help to make them feel more secure and to settle more easily:

- help them pick up the pieces
- get them back to school as soon as you can
- get them to make contact with their family (if that's possible) and friends
- try to get them to talk through with you what has happened
- find out what interests them

They need your help to make sense of what is happening.

Don't be put off if you are rejected at first. Try again. Try a different approach. Gradually they'll come round and want to talk. It may be particularly difficult for young people from different cultures and backgrounds to get their message over.

MEETINGS

Meetings, Meetings, Meetings. There are so many different meetings which often seem to be a waste of time.

Meetings are useful for:

- gaining consensus
- sharing views
- obtaining information
- solving problems
- reaching decisions
- making plans
- checking progress

To be effective meetings need to achieve their aim in a reasonable way in a reasonable time leaving a trail of clear crisp decisions.

Successful meetings depend upon good planning. Detailed plans need to be made before the meeting – who needs to attend and what preparation do they need before taking part. This matters as much as the conduct of the meeting itself.

It is a good idea to go over review forms or details of the meeting with the young person beforehand. Talk about what questions they may want to ask and the best way to do so.

Let them know that their contribution will be welcome and valued. Young people are much more likely to attend the meeting if they can see its' purpose and feel it will be worthwhile.

The following may be useful for whoever is organising the meeting. Items marked with a * apply to whoever is chairing the meeting:

If you do not think a meeting is being organised well, you should contact the chair to discuss your concerns.

1   Time and Date

a) If the meeting is a planning meeting or review then it should be arranged so that the young person can easily attend.

b) Always try to set the date for the next meeting before closing the present meeting if this is possible.

2   Place

Choose a venue that is suitable for the occasion and prepare the room well before the meeting begins so that if anyone arrives early they have somewhere to go.

- how should the chairs and, if needed, any tables be laid out?
- would comfortable chairs and coffee table be better?
- what equipment is needed e.g. tape recorder, flip chart?
- does the meeting need to be on neutral ground?
- is the environment pleasant and suitable for the occasion?
- is access easy?
- is there parking available or is there public transport close by?
- will anyone require transport or their expenses paid in advance?

Agenda

a) This should be prepared and if possible published beforehand. It should identify the topics to be considered and also who is to introduce the subject.*

It is more important to examine the future than to go back over the past.

b) Don't have too many items. A long agenda is tiring and boring and items will not get the attention they deserve.*

c) If the meeting is informal, let those present know what you want to discuss before you begin.*

Time-keeping

a) A prompt start makes good use of the time available. Any delay in starting encourages people to arrive late in the future.

b) Breaks are useful to divide up different topics and prevent boredom. If you are chairing the meeting do control the length of breaks and keep pressure up on progress.*

c) Set a finish time and keep to it. Say what it will be at the beginning of the meeting. We owe it to other people to make the best use of their time.*

d) Announce approximately 10 minutes before the end of the meeting that the meeting is drawing to a close.*

Minutes/Notes

Unfortunately minutes are often used as a form of protection or insurance. They therefore contain a lot about 'who said what'. The importance of minutes is that they record decisions reached and actions planned. In other words who is to do what and by when.

Reviewing minutes of meetings is then confined to checking whether people have done what they promised.

Size of meetings

A meeting needs to be manageable. Large meetings prevent full contributions and become more formal. Small meetings have limited expertise, but are less formal.

One way of keeping attendance to a reasonable number is to have people attend solely for the items which concern them.

The meeting

The carer should help to make sure the young person sits in a suitable place. If the young person wishes, you should sit next to him/her.

Have ready some:

- ideas to encourage the young person to suggest solutions if possible

- strategies to help the young person say what they think

Would providing tea or coffee help the meeting or would it be a distraction? Plan accordingly.

End of the meeting

- make sure the meeting ends with a positive feeling with clearly agreed aims and objectives*

- summarise what has taken place*

- who will do what and by when*

- set the date for the next meeting*

- finish on time*

Young people seem to enjoy organizing meetings. The meetings might be for planning future activities or for discussing changes in how the home might be run. These notes may be helpful for them too!

PLANNING MEETINGS

> Every young person must have an up to date plan so that they know where they stand and what it is hoped will happen to them in the future. They should take part in making this plan which will then have their commitment. In some cases an interpreter may be needed. Your local authority will give you guidance on this.

Sometimes the first planning meeting takes place before the young person leaves home but if not as soon as possible afterwards.

What will be on the plan?

- what the young person's needs are including health, diet, religion, language, education, friends, carers. This may mean finding out where particular shops, selling for example Afro-Caribbean food or say Asian cosmetics, are located

- if a young person is disabled what extra help they need

- where the young person will be living

- if it is possible to predict how long they are likely to be looked after by social services

- what will happen in the future, and when it will happen

- when the young person will see their parent(s), and how the parent(s) will be involved

- what will happen if things don't work out as planned

- arrangements for education and health care

- who is responsible for carrying out the plan

Who goes to a planning meeting?

Whenever possible:

- the young person
- parent(s)
- the social worker
- anyone else who cares about the young person such as grandparents, aunts, uncles, friends
- anyone who works with the young person such as the manager of a children's home
- foster carer/key worker
- other people may be invited such as teachers, doctors, educational welfare officers etc

Can I speak at the meeting?

Encourage the young person to say what they think and to be part of any decisions made.

Young people may ask for their parent(s) to leave the room for a time if they feel uncomfortable speaking in the front of them. Parent(s) can also ask for the young person to leave the room when it is their turn to speak.

What happens next?

The agreed plan and any decisions made in the meeting will be written down and everybody who was invited will be given a copy, including the young person.

Further planning meetings may be called later to see how things are progressing.

As it is not always easy to put the plan into action quickly you will need to tell the young person what is going on as well as encouraging them to follow up anything they are worried about.

REVIEWS

Lots of young people will say reviews are a waste of time but reviews are very important for young people, even though quite often they don't realise it.
They should be encouraged to attend whenever possible and if they can't attend, to send their apologies and any comments they may have.

Whoever is responsible for organising a young person's review should make sure that the time and place is suitable for everyone especially the young person. It is after all **their review**. A young person can if they wish ask for a review to take place.

What are reviews?

Reviews are regular meetings which social services must hold for all young people who are looked after by them.

A review is held:

- to make sure that the plans made for the young person are being carried out

- to decide whether the plans should be changed in any way

How often do they happen?

They are held within 4 weeks of when a young person is first looked after, but they may be held earlier; then within three months; then within six months.

If a lot is happening or there is a problem then reviews may be held more often.

Must I go to them?

It's a very good idea for the young person to attend as they can have their say about what's going on. Encourage the young person to speak up, to moan or make suggestions.

The young person can take a friend or someone they can trust if they wish.

Ref. No: G&R V4 p58-73, V3 p80-86

They can also get that person to speak on their behalf if they find talking in front of everyone difficult, but encourage them to speak up for themselves.

If it really isn't possible for the young person to attend their review they can write down what they want to say and ask someone else to read it for them.

Who will be there?

All the people who are concerned about the young person should be there including their parent(s), carer, social worker and sometimes teacher and/or interpreter.

If at the review the young person doesn't want to say what they feel in front of their parent(s) they can ask for them to leave the room. The parent(s) might also ask for the young person to leave the room whilst they have their say. If it is known that this might happen it is a good idea to tell either the young person or the parent(s) in advance.

What happens before the review?

The young person will be asked, usually to write down, sometimes on a printed form:

- how they are getting on

- what they want to happen in the future

- anything else they would like to talk about at the review

Their social worker and carer will also be asked to write down what they think as well. Everyone should see what the others have written before the review.

Will someone take notes of what is said at the meeting?

Yes and everyone including the young person should get a copy.

If a young person is not happy they should tell you or their social worker. If they feel strongly, encourage them to put their view of what happened in writing and try to get the notes changed.

It's a good idea for the young person to keep their own notes of what happened anyway or to write down the main points afterwards.

Help them to follow up matters if what has been agreed doesn't happen within a reasonable amount of time. The time for something to happen/action to be taken should be agreed at the review.

CHILD PROTECTION CONFERENCE/REGISTER

What is a Child Protection Conference?

This is a meeting called if either social services, the police, a teacher or someone from the health service such as a doctor thinks a young person may be suffering; or at serious risk of suffering, significant harm because of:

- physical injury or neglect or sexual abuse or emotional abuse and may need protection

Who goes to a Child Protection Conference

Any of the following **MAY** attend:

- the young person
- their parent(s)
- their social worker and other social service officials
- the police
- a teacher
- a doctor or someone from the health authority
- if the young person is 'being looked after' their carer may attend

The young person may also bring along a friend or someone they trust just to be there or to speak on their behalf.

A specially trained clerk will also be in attendance to take the minutes.

A member of staff from the social services department usually chairs the meeting.

Who gets a copy of the minutes?

Everyone present at the meeting will get a copy, If the parent(s) are only present for part of the time then they will only be given the minutes of that part of the meeting.

What happens at the meeting?

The first Child Protection Conference is called to exchange information and to decide on whether the young person should be placed on the Child Protection Register. If so, then a keyworker will be appointed to:

- co-ordinate a plan
- help the young person and parent(s) to take part in the plan
- keep the young person informed of what is going on

The plan is made to ensure the young person is kept safe and well and that he/she gets any help they need. The plan will also show any other action that may be necessary.

What is a Child Protection Register?

It is a list of children/young people who are considered to be suffering from or who are likely to suffer significant harm. The reasons for a young person's name appearing on the register should be fully explained to the young person.

Why is there a list?

- to provide a list of all children/young people in the area whom it is thought may be, or who are, definitely at risk

- to provide a central point of reference for professional staff who are worried about a young person and want to know quickly whether a child protection plan exists

- to provide information for all the professionals concerned

When can my name come off the list?

- if the plan made at the Child Protection Conference is successful and it is thought that a young person is no longer at risk

- if the reasons which originally led to the registration no longer apply

- the young person has moved to another area and that area has accepted responsibility for the case

- the young person is 18 years old

- the young person has married

- the young person has died

The first two categories for de-registration always require a conference to take place. All other categories may be agreed without the need for a meeting.

How often do these meetings take place?

They must be held at least every six months to review the situation – more often if necessary until such time as everyone agrees they are no longer required.

For further information, see your Child Protection Procedures.

WORKING WITH PARENT(S)

> The Children Act says that contact between a child who is looked after and his/her family, and those connected with him/her must be encouraged. As far as possible carers should work in partnership with parent(s).
>
> Even if a care order is in force, contact must be encouraged unless the order says otherwise.

Research has shown that a very large number of young people who are looked after return home again, often quite soon (*Going Home, The Return of Children Separated from their Families*, Roger Bullock, Michael Little, Spencer Millham). Keeping contact with families is therefore especially important. It is CRUCIAL to make good links with a young person's family within the first weeks of the young person being looked after. This can determine how often a young person will meet up with the family in the future.

The young person's social worker should draw up a plan, as soon as possible, showing contact with families. If the young person does not have a social worker then the plan should be discussed with the team manager. Some local authorities may have different practises and you should ensure the guidelines are followed.

BAAF have published a useful book "*Contact: Managing Visits to Children Looked After Away from Home*" (see page 177).

A Berkshire foster carer said

> "Partnership with families is the most important part. But it can be difficult when one side of the partnership does not want to take into consideration what the child's wishes are"

On the other hand many young people resent the fact that suddenly parent(s) who have not bothered about them in the past should suddenly be involved in decision making about their lives.

> "When they tell ME it's a good idea to see my family, I tell them where to go!"

As with every good tale, there are two sides to the story. Quite often you, as the carer may feel like 'the pig in the middle'.

- listen to what both sides have to say

- talk to the young person regularly, about all sorts of things. A young person will probably come round to talking about their family at some time

- find out all the facts you can; it may be that you should read the young person's file

- sometimes a brother, sister, grandparent, relative or friend can act as a go-between

- take things slowly, one step at a time. Don't rush

- if you arrange a first meeting, arrange it on neutral ground, a Macdonalds, Pizza Hut or some such place

- if either party refuses to make contact at first, don't give up, but be sensitive to the difficulties

- there will probably be lots of hate/hurt – explain things as you see them to both sides

Most young people really do want contact with parent(s) even if they won't admit it. The following are just two quotes, one from a girl and the other from a boy.

> ..."We should try hard to stick with our families"
>
> ..."At the end of the day everyone has to have contact with their families"

There are practical things that you could do to encourage keeping contact with families. Many are more appropriate for young people living in a children's home:

- when the young person comes to your home, get them to bring their own duvet and/or items from their bedroom if possible. It may help them feel more secure and it will remind them of their home and their families

- parent(s) could be involved with holidays or outings or on committees

- suggest the parent(s) come to the home – if the local authority (or court) agrees

- suggest the young person visits their parent(s) home for a short while, gradually building up to overnight, then a weekend visit – if the local authority (or court) agrees. This contact needs to form part of the young person's overall plan

- once good contact is established parent(s) could be asked to come to the home to help out in a practical way such as wiring up a new stereo system or demonstrating a particular skill they may have

Keeping parent(s) in touch with what is going on in the young person's life is a good way of keeping them informed. It is much easier for parent(s) to work in partnership if they are kept informed.

Once you have got the contact going, you will have to help to keep it going.

You will probably also have to explain to both parties:

- just what 'working in partnership' means in practice
- what the benefits are for both sides
- that talking and discussing are better than arguing and shouting

However, if it really won't work out, have a plan ready so you know how you will handle the situation from both sides.

There may be other important people in a young person's life and they may need help to keep in touch with those people.

Of course there will be set backs, these are only to be expected. Act as a mediator if you can by:

- encouraging the contact
- keeping the contact going
- helping the young person to remember family birthdays
- inviting families to special events
- encouraging telephone contact and letters
- encouraging the exchange of photographs
- being welcoming when families come
- telling parent(s) that their travelling expenses may be paid by the social services department
- sharing information

It is also a good idea for you to keep a record of whenever contact is made between families and the young person.

COLLECTING MEMENTOS

Talking about their past is often a very painful experience for young people and many don't want to do it. Others will be extremely keen to learn as much as they can.

All young people who are looked after will have a past; a present; and a future. Wait until you feel the time is right to talk to the young person about where they have lived, who they have lived with, what memories they have and what more they would like to know.

Collecting mementos is a way of filling in the jigsaw of a young person's life, both in the past and for the future.

They may bring with them mementos that are important to them, or they may, out of choice, bring nothing, hoping to wipe out bitter memories. On the other hand they may have nothing to bring.

What is a treasure to one young person may be trash to another. Respecting personal possessions may be a hard lesson for some young people to learn, but one worth learning.

Everyone will be different and all your skill will be needed in this area.

You could keep an envelope handy for them where you or they can pop in mementos or photos and keep them safe.

It's also worth keeping a good filing system going of negatives and of photographs taken, as it can be disappointing for the young person when they decide they want to remember a particular event, and the negatives can't be found!

IT IS IMPORTANT THAT YOUNG PEOPLE LEAVE THEIR PLACEMENT WITH POSITIVE MEMORIES.

Some young people may wish to do some Life Story Work so the next sheet gives some more details.

LIFE STORY WORK

Life story work is a way of giving young people a chance to learn about their past life and history. It should help them to understand some of the things that have happened. Often the information is put together safely into an album which may be called a life book. This work is normally done by a specialist who may be a social worker. On page 177 there are details of a book entitled "Life Story Work" published by BAAF.

But I know all about me!

- 'you might think you do but often your memory, or what you have been told, is not correct'
- 'will you remember when you are an adult?'
- 'who will be around to tell you?'

Some information will be on social services file but things like photographs and keepsakes need to be put together whilst they can still be found. Sadly though, information sometimes just cannot be found.

How long will it take to do?

That depends on whoever is doing life story work with the young person – but it might be once a week for say an hour or two. It depends on whether they will be going out to take photographs, make visits or whether it is just a question of organising what is already there.

Some ideas might be drawing family trees; tracing maps; putting photographs into an album; writing down memories after a chat; visiting cemeteries to look at gravestones.

It all depends on how much the young person wants to include or how much research they want to do.

Must I do it?

Everyone has a right to privacy so of course the answer is "No". Often young people who have left care say they wish they had done it.

When they are older they will know things about themselves which they will be able to share with their own family and friends.

Whose book is it?

It belongs to the young person but you may offer to keep it in a safe place as photographs and keepsakes cannot be replaced. But it really is up to the young person what they do with it and to whom they show it.

It is also a good idea to add to it with photographs and mementos of the young person's time being looked after.

COMPLAINTS

One area of the Children Act that has caused much worry is the requirement for social services departments to have a complaints procedure (this is called the representation procedure). This shouldn't be so. Making a complaint should be seen as a positive step.

It means the young person has:

- thought about the situation

- decided that something is not right

- is willing to do something about it

There are two different types of complaints.

1. The really serious ones which must be handled formally.

2. Those which can be handled within the home, such as moans, suggestions and problems.

What may seem unimportant to you may be very serious to a young person.

Complaints about sexual or racial harassment or racial discrimination are important. You may be able to help or you may have to take the matter further.

Everyone should know what the complaints procedure is and how they go about making a complaint. If the information is not available the young person should be told how to get hold of the procedure.

Carers in children's homes and foster carers will have their own complaints procedure which may not be the same as the one for young people.

Homes that encourage criticism and comment will be better places in which to live – there's always room for improvement everywhere. It is healthy for moans to be discussed openly and everyone's point of view heard.

> A children's home manager said "We've only had 30 complaints this month". She was disappointed. She saw complaints from young people as a way of improving the care and service provided and of making the home a better place for the young people to live.

If the complaint is of a serious nature then the correct formal procedure for your authority must be followed.

You should keep the young person informed of what is going on and let them know the outcome of the complaint.

Many young people feel that it is not worth making a complaint either because they might be victimised or because the system is stacked against them:

- reassure them on both counts
- help them work out what they want to say
- support them in what they are trying to do

Of course, you may not feel able to help them for all sorts of reasons. You should then put them in touch with someone who can. These might be:

- senior members of staff
- Citizen's Advice Bureaux
- local councillors
- ombudsmen
- the courts – young people can ask for a judicial review

Some hints for handling a complaint:

1. Listen attentively to the young person's complaint. Make sure you fully understand it, take notes.

2. Show that you understand his/her feelings and thank him/her for raising the matter.

3. State your own position undefensively and without hostility.

4. Find out if the young person has any suggestions for resolving the complaint.

5. If appropriate, say what you will do to correct the situation

6. Always set a specific follow-up date.

7. Always give them a copy of your notes or a copy of the formal complaint.

DISCRIMINATION

What does discrimination mean?

The dictionary definition is: "to treat differently because of prejudice"

Is discrimination against the law?

The Sex Discrimination Act 1975 and the Race Relations Act 1976 provide some protection for people on the grounds of gender or race but there is no legal discriminatory protection for gay people. There is only a small amount of protection for people with disabilities – Disabled Persons (Employment) Act 1944 and 1958.

What are the main types of discrimination?

The Council for Racial Equality give the following definitions:

" **Direct discrimination**. Direct discrimination happens when you are treated worse than others or segregated from them, because of your race, colour, nationality, or ethnic or national origins.

Indirect discrimination. This is more complicated. It happens when everyone seems to be treated in the same way, but, in practice, people from a certain ethnic group are put at a greater disadvantage. The law says that when a rule hits a particular ethnic group harder than others (intentionally or not) – and there's no good reason for the rule – it is indirectly discriminatory.

Victimisation. If you are victimised because you have complained about racial discrimination, or because you have supported someone else's complaint, this, too, is unlawful discrimination.

Discrimination applies to:
Jobs
Training
Housing
Education
Services – from councils, banks, insurance companies, pubs, clubs, discos, restaurants, cinemas, travel agencies and so on."

It is important to realize that some people belong to more than one discriminated against group e.g. they may be black and disabled.

Why do people discriminate?

Some people discriminate because they do not like a particular group or situation. Many people discriminate without realizing it.

Most young black people in this country have British Nationality and have the same rights as everyone else. White young people often don't understand this. There are comparatively few black people living in this country (about 6% of the population), so when white young people from mainly white areas meet black people for the first time it can come as quite a culture shock.

Discrimination doesn't just mean treating someone differently, it also includes using names, or words, no matter how innocently, which put people down. If you hear name calling going on, ensure you discuss it. All too often young people don't realize how hurtful and cruel they are being.

Am I black or am I white?

"Am I black or am I white?
I used to ask that question
every day and night
why do you ask a question
as obvious as that?
It's plain to see that you are black

But being in care
In a white Community
It's hard to decide
with no black family"

These are the first two verses of a poem by Margaret Parr published in Chapter 1, Black Experiences of Improving Practice with Children and Families. It highlights the problems of a black young person being cared for by white carers.

What does the Children Act say?

The Children Act says that due consideration should be made to the young person's religious persuasion, racial origin, cultural and linguistic background. Where young people are disabled the local authority must provide services to help the disabled to lead the lives they wish.

What this means is:

Recognizing differences

Differences should not be ignored. People are not all the same. Some people have different skin colour, hair, religious backgrounds. They may practise different rites in relation to their culture. Some young people have different languages. Some young people may be in a wheelchair or have a speech impediment.

Respecting differences

No one should be discriminated against because of their difference. Young people may need your help to learn to respect differences.

Meeting racial, disability, religious, cultural, dietary and cosmetic needs

Young people may previously have been living with their own (natural) families or have been looked after away from their families.

As their carer, you will need to find out what the young person has been used to and what practices they would like to follow.

The young person may have strong views on whether or not they want for example to eat Asian or Caribbean food; attend a Mosque or West Indian Church; wear their hair in a particular way; be treated differently because of their disability.

The young person may:

- want to know where to buy certain foods or cream for their hair/skin

- need to buy braille paper or find out how to get access to different places if they are in a wheelchair

- need support and help to explore different possibilities for their life

- need help so they feel confident about asking for and getting help

Supporting these young people

Sometimes young people may suffer harassment because of their skin colour, religion, disability, sexuality, or indeed because they are 'in care'. They need help and guidance in all sorts of ways, for example on how to complain and who to complain to.

Building pride and esteem

All young people need positive images of themselves, their background and way of life.

How carers can help

- find out all you can about the background/history/culture of any young person who lives with you. It may be something you could do together. Local libraries are a good starting point for this research, so is talking to the young person

- discuss with the young person what food they like to eat and then explore together the shops that sell such foods

- organise a meeting with other members of staff/young people to exchange information and ideas

- find out the names and addresses of local groups where young people can meet other people of their own culture/religion or other disabled young people if they wish

- if a young person feels they are being discriminated against you could help them make a complaint. They could contact any of the following:

CAB – Citizens Advice Bureaux or local advice and information centres

Commission for Racial Equality

Area office of social services department

Equal Opportunities Commission

Some local councils have set up offices (sometimes called Equal Opportunity Units) to deal with discrimination in housing, employment etc.

Schools and colleges

Church, Gurudaware, Mosque, Hindu temple – will have people who are keen to speak to young people. Some have liaison workers

Youth centres/youth counselling services

Personnel manager, the person responsible for staff or the trade union representative if the young person is at work

---

DISCRIMINATION SHOULD BE CHALLENGED AT EVERY LEVEL AT ALL TIMES

Ref. No: G&R V4 p43, 46 V3 p7, 11

PLACES TO LIVE

Before a young person is looked after there should have been a planning meeting and all the necessary arrangements made.

The aim, in most, but not all, cases will be to get a young person back living with their parent(s) or guardian(s) as soon as possible.

Wherever they live young people need to know what to expect and what the rules of the house are.

Honestly tell them what the present situation is, such as how long they will be staying, whether they will be fostered short term or long term, etc.

Many young people will definitely want to be fostered or definitely will not, preferring to live in a children's home. Their social worker should tell them about the options.

With the help of their social worker, if they have one, encourage the young person to visit the local children's homes, foster carer(s), or other future placements; to speak to the young people there and the carers – the young person will be better able to make informed choices about where they would like to live.

Being fostered, what does is mean?

It means a young person (and hopefully any brothers and sisters) will be looked after by another person, called a foster carer in the foster carer's own home. This may be either for a short time while things are sorted out at home or for a longer period, depending on the situation.

Can anyone be a foster carer?

No, anyone can apply but they are carefully chosen.

What happens?

Once the young person has decided they would like to be fostered, social services will try to find a foster carer who is suitable:

- has the same background and racial origin

- has the same religion (if they have one)

- understands their needs

- lives close by so they can attend the same school

- has other children in their family or does not have any children depending on the young person's needs

The young person will visit the carer's house, perhaps several times. The young person and the carer then decide whether they think they will be suitable for each other. Once this is agreed social services will make all the necessary arrangements.

The foster family will do what they think is best and will treat the young person as part of their family. Their social worker/key worker should call regularly.

If the foster family is from a different racial background the social worker or whoever is responsible will try to ensure the young person has contact with people of similar background.

Although every care is taken to make a young person's stay with a foster family successful, sometimes it just does not work out. This may be through no fault of anyone; circumstances may change or a young person who thought they would like to be fostered finds out that it is not for them.

Children's homes, what are they?

These are houses of varying sizes that are run by social services or organisations like Barnardos or Catholic Children's homes.

They try to provide young people who cannot live at home with the best possible quality of life in the circumstances.

The home will be run by a team of staff, usually led by a manager. There will be staff on duty on a rota basis 24 hours a day, 365 days a year.

Sometimes the home will be separated into sections so that part of it will be made into small flats, often called Independent Units where young people can learn skills such as budgeting and cooking to help them prepare for when they are no longer 'looked after'.

A keyworker is normally allocated to each young person who should also have a social worker. If this is not the case then the keyworker may be asked to undertake some social work duties such as acting as advocate for the young person on a temporary basis.

In many homes the house rules are set in partnership with the young people.

The young person will be encouraged to attend school/college/work regularly, to bring friends to the home and to act responsibly around the house.

Sometimes their stay will be short lived and they can go back to living with their parent(s).

Secure units, what are they?

Secure units are buildings specially designed for young people whose liberty needs to be restricted.

Some secure accommodation will be attached to a children's home. Others will be located separately.

It may be necessary for a young person to be housed in secure accommodation outside their area if there are no facilities or vacancies locally.

No one under the age of 13 years may be placed in secure accommodation without the permission of the Secretary of State.

No one can be kept in a secure unit for more than 72 hours over any one period of 28 days without a court order.

When might I be sent to a secure unit?

There are very severe regulations on when a young person's liberty can be restricted.

If the young person has NOT committed an offence, under the Children Act 1989 the young person will only be placed in secure accommodation if:

(i) the young person has a history of absconding and is likely to abscond from any other type of accommodation

   and if the young person absconds, he/she is likely to suffer significant harm

(ii) if the young person is kept in any other type of accommodation he/she is likely to injure themselves or other people

The court cannot, send a young person to secure accommodation. Application must still be made by the local authority – Children (Secure Accommodation) Regulations 1991. When the Criminal Justice Act is fully implemented (probably May 1995), the court will have the power to send young offenders to secure accommodation.

The only other reason for a young person being placed in secure accommodation is under the Mental Health Act 1983.

Secure orders are permissive orders. This means that they allow for a gradual rehabilitation of the young person into the community.

A young person placed in secure accommodation will have all normal rights except freedom to leave the building.

THE HOME ENVIRONMENT

The best children's home I ever visited had been the family house of the home manager and her husband which had been converted to a children's home.

It felt like a home, it looked like home. It was home to all the residents, both long term and short term stayers, and as such was respected by them.

The environment in which we all live is really important, much more important than many realize. A young person said that although the staff seemed nicer at a particular home she wouldn't go there because "It was a mess – how could I take my friends to a place like that?"

It is important to involve young people in how the home is organised and decorated as this will help them establish an identity; a sense of belonging.

What can I do around the house?

Involve young people in:

- choosing colour schemes

- where possible in actually decorating, not just their room but other parts of the house

- choosing any new furniture, equipment or pictures

- changing the layout of different parts of the house

- taking responsibility for the care and cleaning of the house/their room

What can I do in my room?

They should have their own room:

- if that's not possible their own space in an agreed part of a room where they can put up pictures, posters etc

- let them be responsible for keeping it clean and tidy

- if they are sharing, let them agree the ground rules with the other occupant

Ref. No: G&R V4 p14 (esp 1.171)

- give them a key to their room. Only go in their room when they are not there if it is essential
- young disabled people should be helped to live a full life. You may have to make changes around the home

Things that may seem unimportant at the time may have more of an impact than you think.

- if something gets broken or damaged, don't just leave it or call in the expert to do the job. If possible, work with the young person who caused the damage or any others interested in putting it right. They'll respect it more next time
- a few indoor plants here and there will give a good feeling to a home – possibly grown by the young people, and certainly nurtured by them
- let them cut the grass or hoe the flower beds

    Not only will they be learning life skills but will get the satisfaction from a job well done and be able to admire the results of their efforts

- if food is set out with care it seems to taste much better. If you set standards many young people will learn what is possible and remember it for the future
- everyone, whether male or female, should try to make that little extra effort with the way they look. Set an example. The young people will notice. They may laugh at you or compliment you but they will notice. You'll set a standard for them to follow

It is all part of building up their confidence, making them feel important and making them feel they are taking part in decisions, no matter how small that affect their lives.

MONEY

> "The way allowances work does not help the young people to get a sense of reality" – carer
>
> "If you don't ask you don't get it" – young person
>
> "It ought to be written down the money you're entitled to" – young person
>
> "I share with the young people how much money we have. I think the reality that there is only so much money available is useful for them to know" – children's home manager

Young people and carers agree that:

- learning to manage money is an important skill

- knowing what is available and how it is shared out is important – it gives them a sense of reality

- young people should be told what everyone is entitled to and why. It will help them understand why some young people seem to get more than others

- young people need to know so they can make choices in their day to day lives

- young people should be involved in decision making on how the money is spent so they can learn to plan for their future

Some local authorities give clear guidelines on how money should be allocated and spent. Others leave it to the discretion of foster carers, home managers, social workers and even area managers.

Whatever the system, young people need to be told about it; to be told what they will get both now and in the future; and they need to be involved in deciding how any special allowances are spent. They may also need your help to get it!

A young man from Birmingham was very upset because his carer had decided, without consultation with him, that his special needs allowance should be spent on a personal stereo and tapes of his native language, Punjabi. He desperately wanted a pair of special trainers similar to those worn by the rest of his basketball team.

- he gave up playing in the team because he was too embarrassed to wear his own trainers

- he flatly refused to listen to the tapes

- he was very angry and resentful

The carer, with the best will in the world was giving "due consideration" to the child's religious persuasion, racial origin, cultural and linguistic background" but not considering the rights and responsibilities of that young person.

This is a difficult area as someone will always feel unjustly treated but if money matters are discussed freely then young people will know what to expect and when.

Special circumstances for giving extra money should be kept to a minimum.

Local authorities are now required to provide money for young people who wish to further their education and for those young people 'leaving care'.

- find out exactly what money is available

- work hard to make sure they get it

- make sure young people are treated fairly

- make sure young people know well in advance what they can expect

They'll thank you for it!

> Money matters must be seen to be fair.

MANAGING MONEY/BUDGETING/SAVING

'My friends think I'm better off being in care' and, of course, they may be right from a material point of view. It would seem to an outsider that there is an allowance for everything – a new bike, for outings, school trips, for hobbies and clothes.

Learning how to manage money is important to everyone. Young people who are living in a children's home or a foster home will need special help in this area as their circumstances may never be quite the same again.

Keeping a budget plan is a good idea to help them manage their money. On page 41 is one they might like to use.

Money – what do I need to think about?

- what they need each week
- where the money will come from
- whether it will cover their expenses
- if it won't, what they can do about it

Young people also need to learn about the reasons and importance of saving money and the different methods available to them.

Even the cleverest person sometimes gets in a muddle with money so it's important that young people understand how difficult budgeting is and that they get plenty of practice before becoming independent.

Everyone's needs are different so is what is important to them. Here are a few ideas on how you could help young people to save on outgoings: The list is based on one produced in "Stepping Out" by the NFCA.

Ref. No: G&R V4 p21-23, 108, 111, V3 p9-10, 38, 98

How can I cut down on my expenses?

- buy clothes that last and won't go out of fashion too quickly
- buy clothes at sale time
- don't buy clothes which are 'dry clean only', they are expensive to clean
- washing clothes by hand is cheaper than the launderette or washing machine
- walk, if possible, rather than use bus/car/train – it's healthier and saves money
- use a bike – buy a second-hand one from adverts in newspapers or go to auctions
- use the library for books, CDs, cassettes and videos
- avoid late-night corner shops, because, although they tend to be convenient, they are expensive
- Buy groceries etc in bulk with friends. If they're becoming independent soon perhaps its something a group could do together
- cook for friends – take it in turns – it's often cheaper and gives more variety
- get a season ticket if the young person travels regularly
- car boot sales, jumble sales, markets and auctions can provide good cheap finds, whether it's clothing, furniture, books or other household goods
- get a free hair cut by being a model on a training night at the local hairdressers or training school
- keep heating bills down by making sure there is draft excluder around doors and windows
- wear more clothes rather than turn up the heating
- make phone calls after 6.00 pm or at weekends, it's cheaper
- ready-cooked and take-away food can be expensive, so try cooking more meals
- avoid buying things on the doorstep or through mail-order catalogues, because it can get expensive and out of control
- fresh vegetables are cheap to buy and very nourishing
- buying meat from a local butcher is often cheaper than supermarkets and they usually sell cheaper cuts as well
- avoid buying goods on credit or H.P. – it's expensive

Should a young person get into debt, they will also need to know where they can go for help and advice. Is there a debt counsellor in your area? Is there someone from social services who could help?

> Giving up or reducing smoking is not just good for Health but it is an excellent way of saving money!

MANAGING MONEY/BUDGETING/SAVING – CHECKLIST

FILL IN THESE CHARTS TO WORK OUT WHERE YOUR MONEY IS GOING

OUTGOINGS	WEEKLY	MONTHLY	YEARLY
Rent			
Food			
Travel			
Clothes			
TV Licence and/or rental			
Council Tax			
Water Rates			
Electricity			
Gas			
Laundry			
Cleaning materials			
Soap, make up, deodorant etc.			
Drink			
Cigarettes			
Presents			
Entertainment			
Credit/HP/Loans			
Other			
Total			

(NFCA)

INCOME	WEEKLY	MONTHLY	YEARLY
Take-home pay			
Benefits			
Housing Benefits			
Other			
Total			

INCOME	WEEKLY	MONTHLY	YEARLY
Income			
Outgoings			
WHAT'S LEFT?			

NOTES

EDUCATION

Education is a good way to build a sound future. Lots of recent research about young people has shown how worried they are about their education. Young people really need your help to get the best from education.

Young people were worried that:

- they were getting behind with their work because of poor attendance

- this often made them not want to go to school which makes matters worse

- their concentration was not as good as it should be – worries, disturbances or neglect may well be the cause

- they had frequent changes of schools

- the time it took to get them into a school after a move was too long – it is recommended that this should not be more than 3 days

- they were not getting enough extra help to enable them to catch up

- home tutoring was not available soon or often enough if there was a problem with school

- quite often there was no place that was quiet where they could do their homework

- sometimes they were treated differently at school

- if they were disabled they might have problems moving about the building. Sometimes they might be teased

They need your help. Here are some ideas other carers have suggested:

- make a nuisance of yourself with the education office to get things speeded up, in order to get a young person back into school or being home tutored or anything else that may be needed

- help them, possibly without the other young people knowing, so they don't lose face, with their weaker subjects such as reading or spelling

- if you don't feel you can help them with their homework/schoolwork find someone else who can help them

- encourage them, praise them, and show an interest in all they do

- if the young person is disabled make sure the school has suitable access facilities. You may also have to help to get them into the school building

- make sure there is a place set aside especially for homework

A very few young people will find that the education system does not meet their needs. Work based alternatives may be the answer. The social services person responsible for education will advise you.

The question of feeling that they are being treated differently because of where they are living is not a new one. It may be lack of understanding or genuine concern but if it is upsetting the young person then you may need to go to the school to try to sort out the problem.

GSCE examinations include a good deal of course work so if a young person changes school at 14, 15 or 16 years they may not be able to take all their exams. It is especially important that 'all the stops' are pulled out to try to get the young person to stay at the same school.

There may also be other ways of getting round problems of changing school and missing class work. Ask the education office.

On the next pages are some questions that could apply to any young person. Take the time to go over the points with them and the changes in their school life will be much smoother and less of a worry.

> For young people not to be educated is not acceptable. If you or the young person's social worker don't get anywhere, the following can be contacted.
>
> YOUR LOCAL COUNCILLOR
> THE SOCIAL SERVICES PERSON RESPONSIBLE FOR LIAISON WITH EDUCATION
> THE EDUCATION OFFICE
> IN FACT ANYONE YOU THINK MIGHT HELP

EDUCATION – A YOUNG PERSON'S CHECKLIST

Moving to another home doesn't necessarily mean you have to change schools, but sometimes you will have to choose another school to go to.

Most people change schools around their 11th birthday anyway, when they change from junior school to senior school.

If I have to change schools how do I choose my new school?

There may not be much choice, depending on where you live, but if you have to choose a new school, your carer can go with you to look round a few schools. Talk to the teachers and pupils and then decide, providing there is a vacancy.

What will it be like starting a new school?

Some things may be done differently.

- everyone takes time to settle in somewhere new
- ask if you're not sure about anything
- talk any problems over with your carer or your friends

How do I choose which subjects to study?

When a young person is 13 or 14 they will have to decide which subjects they want to study until they are 16. These are their GCSE subjects. At school they usually take two years' study.

You will be given talks on the subjects you can do and will probably have hand-outs to read. Think about:

- how interesting will the subjects be
- will they help you get the job you want
- will there be a lot of reading to do
- will there be a lot of practical things to do

You won't have a completely free choice because:

- the law says you have to learn certain subjects such as Maths and English
- some subjects may clash on the school timetable

What can I do when I'm 16?

You can go:

- on to get more qualifications such as A levels or GNVQ,
- start a skills course at college such as bricklaying, gardening or word processing
- find a job or start on a training scheme
- improve your maths and English by taking courses in say, number power and word power

Why should I stay on at school or college?

- many jobs need trained workers
- pay and prospects are likely to be better after further study
- you will have a wider choice of jobs or careers

What qualifications will I need?

For some courses you will need to get certain grades in your GCSE subjects. For others you will only have to show you want to work hard.

What if I fail some of my GCSEs?

You can re-take most GCSEs you fail – many people spend an extra year doing this – but it might be better for you to do a vocational (job-related) course instead. Your school or college will help you decide.

How long do courses last?

- GCE A and AS levels courses last two years. GNVQ courses may last two years or make take longer
- most GCSE and NVQ courses last for one year when taken at college. NVQs may take longer depending on the experience, ability and particular circumstances of the young person

You can apply to any college or school you wish but help with transport expenses will only be given in certain cases. Visit with your carer several different places where you could go, and find the one that suits you best.

What will it be like?

There will be more work than when you were doing GCSEs and a lot of it will have to be done in your own time.

It will be hard work and you should expect this, but you will also find you are treated more like an adult than when you were at school.

At college there will be all sorts of different people of all ages over 16. It will take a lot of getting used to. Stick at it and get the qualifications you really deserve.

Young people who have disabilities may take examinations that have been adapted to meet a particular disability e.g. braille question paper or be given extra time in which to complete the examination paper

Most schools/colleges will nominate a particular teacher, for example a year tutor, who will be responsible for you. They will have a supportive/liaising role. They will be the person to contact if there is a problem. This teacher will be responsible for the your emotional, and social development as well as your educational development.

If you have been out of school for some time it may be possible for the school to allow you phased re-introduction into school life.

> Teachers are really pleased when carers come into school to see them. They want carers to work with teachers to improve the education of all young people.

QUALIFICATIONS

Adults and young people alike are often confused by the different qualifications available.

The following is a brief explanation of some of the more usual qualifications:

What are GCSEs?

GCSE stand for General Certificate of Secondary Education and shows that someone has reached a certain standard of school work.

GCSEs may be a mixture of coursework, practical work and studying in own time (homework). There are also exams at the end of the course. GCSEs take two years of study at school but at college they may take one year.

There are 5 grades of GCSE, grade A - E.

What can I do when I finish GCSEs?

Look for a job, study further at college or start on an employment training scheme.

NVQs (National Vocational Qualifications) and GNVQs (General National Vocational Qualifications), what are they?

These are two new ways of achieving qualifications.

NVQs are usually undertaken whilst working although sometimes it is possible to be credited with some parts whilst at college. NVQs may be started at 16 years.

GNVQ qualifications are designed to be college based either full time or part time.

NVQs and GNVQs are made up of a series of units, some compulsory and some that may be chosen. The number of units and the difficulty will depend on the level. The units can be taken all at once or over any period of time with breaks in between units if appropriate.

There are no examinations to be sat for NVQs. The ability to do a task at a certain level is all that is required. An assessor is appointed to confirm the level of competence.

Written tests and internal assessments are used for GNVQ.

Some work that students may study from 14+ onwards (KS4 on chart) may be used as credits for GNVQs which can be started any time from 16 years onwards.

NVQs can be achieved in the following job areas:

Tending animals, plants and land; Extracting and providing natural resources; Construction; Engineering; Manufacturing; Transporting; Providing goods and services; Providing health, social care and protective services; Providing business services; Communicating; Developing and extending knowledge and skill.

At present GNVQs are available in Art & Design; Health & Social Care; Manufacturing; Business; Leisure & Tourism. It is hoped that many other areas will be available shortly.

The awarding bodies for NVQ and GNVQ are City & Guilds, RSA and BTEC Examinations Boards.

Young people with special needs

NVQs have many advantages for young people with special needs because they are:

- flexible

- have no built-in restrictions on how long they should take

- credits may be achieved at any time and gradually built up to make 1 unit

- extra help and resources can be made available

A levels (Advanced Levels)

A levels are the traditional way of getting a place at university or institute of higher education.

When applying for a job at 18, A levels will show an employer that a certain high standard has been reached.

The number of A levels a young person takes will partly depend on GCSE grades, some of which will need to be Grade C or above. Most students take 3 A levels but the school or college will advise on the most appropriate subjects and numbers to take.

AS (Advanced Supplementary) Studies

The standard of AS is as high as A levels but there is only half the amount to study. A levels and A/S levels can be combined.

Both A and AS courses involve a large amount of reading and writing as well as practical work, discussions, field work, lectures and visits.

Although there are exams to take at the end of A and AS levels, the standard of work throughout the course will play an important part in deciding the final result.

BTEC Higher National

These courses are for students aged 18+ and are similar to degree courses.

Degree courses

These are usually studied for three or four years at university.

The qualifications needed to begin a degree course vary from course to course, but a student usually needs some GCSEs and two or three A levels or equivalents as shown on the chart.

Teachers and careers advisers can advise about which courses to take.

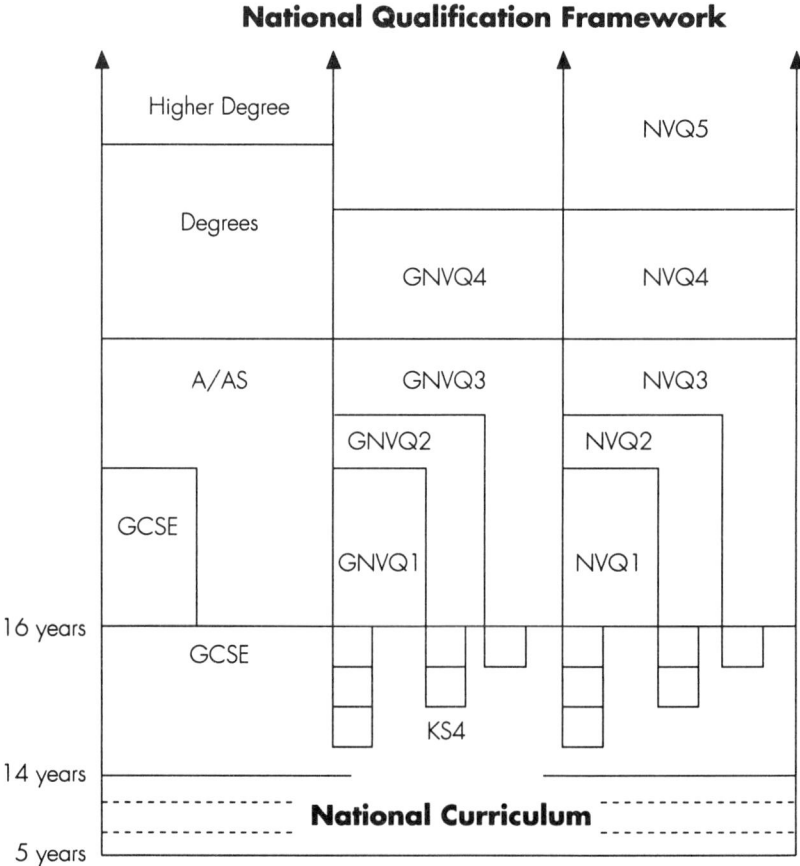

Note: KS4 is a key stage in the National Curriculum, teachers can give more details.

LEISURE - WHAT TO DO IN FREETIME

"Nothing succeeds like success"

Young people will find life more fun if they have interests outside the home.

It will:

- help them build self confidence
- give them a purpose, something to aim for, to achieve
- help them make new friends
- give them somewhere different to go. This is especially important when they 'leave care'

Many young people will need a lot of help and encouragement to begin with.

I like sport, what can I do?

Many towns have swimming pools, skating rinks, sports and leisure centres, tennis courts, five-a-side football pitches etc. The young person could use any of these or join a team and play football, basketball, netball, volleyball etc. There are sports that disabled young people can take part in, such as wheelchair basketball, hockey or tennis.

I like music, what can I do?

They could:

- learn to play a musical instrument
- form or join a band
- make a tape
- go to gigs or concerts

I like 'arty' things, what can I do?

They could:

- paint, draw, act, make music, or just listen or watch
- join clubs for photography, stamp collecting, etc

- go to art galleries or museums

- look for leaflets in their local library about classes, exhibitions or clubs, or go to their local arts centre and talk to the people there

and many other things.

Can I join a club?

Youth clubs, guides and scouts offer lots of different activities; they're a good way of making new friends and they don't cost very much. The local youth service may be helpful in putting black young people in touch with others and **in** helping disabled young people to take part in their chosen activities by advising them on access to the various clubs etc.

What else is there to do?

- young people could attend a church, mosque, synagogue. They will meet many new people and make new friends

- if young people don't want to go to a club or take part in sport, there are plenty of other things they can do, such as reading, making their own clothes, cooking or woodworking. Try getting them to learn a new skill

- there are countryside and environmental projects to take part in or visit

- it is worth visiting village halls, community schools and community centres to find out what is going on there

- go rock climbing, scrambling, abseiling; go on adventure holidays

To find out more there will be leaflets at:

- the local library
- the local arts centre
- sports or leisure centre
- education office
- community offices

The young person may feel too shy to join a club. Why not ask a friend to go with them?

Tell them it can be fun when they start something new – and it will give them something to talk about with their friends, or with adults, or at job or college interview.

Doing something in their spare time can help when they apply for a job.

For example if they were a member of a netball team or football team it could show that they:

- were reliable – turning up for each match
- were punctual
- could follow the rules
- got on well with others
- could work as part of a team
- had leadership qualities
- had self-discipline
- made a regular commitment

Do they know where the information on leisure activities is kept in your home? Is there a file for everyone to use?

I don't want to do anything!

It requires considerable confidence to try something new. Remember those fears "Will I make a fool of myself"? Some young people may have had their self-esteem so battered by their experiences that they may want to stay in bed all day or mope around. Your motivation skills may be sorely tried before a young person takes up a new interest. An invitation to come and see rather than come and sign up is often the best approach.

HEALTH

Good health is important to everyone. Gradually young people must learn to take responsibility for their own health.

Why is good health important?

Because:
- if the young people are ill or have an accident they'll get better more quickly
- they'll probably get ill less often anyway
- they'll be better able to cope with stress
- they'll probably do better at school – an old saying is 'A sound mind in a sound body'
- they'll have less time off school or work so they'll make better progress

What can I do to keep healthy?

1. **Exercise** – Everyone needs exercise because it will help stamina, strength and overall fitness.

   It will help their heart and lungs to work better, stop flabby muscles, keep weight down and generally help them cope with life better.

2. **Sleep** – No two people need exactly the same amount of sleep but regular sleep is essential. Get young people to work out what's best for them.

3. **Noise** – Having very loud music in their ears from a personal stereo really can damage their hearing, and so can loud music in a disco or club. This hearing loss cannot be put right later.

4. **Diet** – This doesn't just mean losing weight. It means thinking about what they eat, how much they eat and why they need certain foods.

   Some foods that are good are:
   fresh fruit and vegetables, pasta, wholemeal bread, low fat milk, unsaturated margarine, white meat, fish

   Some foods that can be bad are:
   crisps, chocolate, sweets, cakes, fizzy drinks

   It's not as bad as it sounds! Together you can experiment with different recipes. The 'bad' foods are not of course forbidden, but it is a good idea to cut down on the amount of these a young person eats and drinks; to grill food instead of frying and to reduce the amount of sugar and salt a young person eats.

   If a young person is, or wishes to become, a vegetarian, care has to be taken to ensure a balanced diet. The Vegetarian Society or your GP will give details.

5. **Weight** – Find out what a young person's ideal weight is and try to get them to stay somewhere near that – sometimes easier said than done! A doctor or nurse will tell them what their weight should be, and weighing machines in chemists shops usually have a chart.

6. **Eating disorders** – This is the term used to describe
   a) anorexia nervosa with sufferers known as anorexic (not eating) and
   b) bulimia nervosa with sufferers known as bulimics (eating too much and then making themselves sick or taking laxatives to clear out the bowels).

   Actually they are not really disorders of eating; rather they indicate and express a person's feelings about themselves.

   9 out of 10 people showing signs of eating disorders are women, the peak age being between 15 and 18 years.

   Many specialists believe the two disorders are part of the same illness. In fact, bulimics have often been anorexics first.

   Eating disorders are emotional disorders which focus on food and consumption. People who suffer may have:

   - a fear of becoming fat

   - a drive to become thin

   - an obsession with food, weight, calories etc

   - a reliance on eating and/or refusal to eat in order to cope with emotional discomfort, stress or developmental changes

   - a view that the world values appearances over personality

Ref No: G&R V4 p107-108 V3 p98

Research has shown that young people who suffer from eating disorders may have been easy children who did not answer back; made less fuss and got less angry. They are often good students and high achievers; anxious to please and to live up to other people's expectations of them.

They are often very secretive and try to hide their illness.

Stress, anxiety, loneliness and depression may trigger off the illness.

If you think there is a problem the young person should contact their GP or the Eating Disorders Association. They may need your help to do this.

7. **Periods** – Many young girls will start their periods at 10 or 11 years of age, others will start much later. Whenever it is they need to be prepared, both physically and mentally. They need to know about:

- sanitary towels and tampons – they should always have a packet stored in their bedroom so they are ready for the start of their periods

- period pains

- vaginal discharge that starts sometime before their periods begin

- the many bodily changes that will be occurring at that time

Help them to look forward to this new phase in their life.

There are many myths and different beliefs surrounding puberty both from a cultural and religious point of view. The Commission for Racial Equality has specialists who can advise you if you need further information.

8. **Personal Hygiene** – Make sure young people know about the need to wash thoroughly and use a deodorant at least once a day. They should also wash their hands after using the toilet.

Changing into clean clothes regularly is essential. Young people also need to be told of the consequences if they don't!

With the changes that take place in both boys and girls during puberty it is particularly important that personal hygiene is stressed.

9. **Smoking** – 'smoking kills' 'smoking causes cancer'.

These are just two statements that must now be printed on cigarette packets as a warning.

The biggest single thing in anyone's life they can do to prevent heart disease is to not smoke, or to give up smoking.

There is a lot of pressure for young people to smoke – from their peers, from films and TV and from older people they admire. It is illegal for young people under 16 to buy cigarettes or tobacco.

Education about the dangers of smoking is a MUST for everyone. Too often smoking is seen as a normal part of growing up without anyone realizing the harm it causes. It is addictive, so giving up will not be easy. It is also expensive.

Reducing or giving up smoking should be encouraged. Don't preach, just encourage – the decision must be their own. You could agree a programme to give up smoking with them and help them stick to it.

10. **Passive smoking** is breathing other people's cigarette smoke. Until recently most people were unaware of the dangers. Not only can it cause irritation to eyes, nose and throat; headaches; dizziness and sickness; it can cause asthma and allergies to worsen and increase the risk of cancer by up to 30%.

In reality many young people who are looked after are smokers. They are often physically and emotionally dependent on cigarettes so it may be necessary to work with the young people to set permissible boundaries that are acceptable to smokers and non-smokers alike.

HOUSE RULES ON SMOKING MUST BE KEPT BY EVERYONE

11. **Alcohol** – Like tobacco, alcohol is a drug. As with all drugs, if it is not used sensibly it can cause problems. Drinking too much alcohol can damage health.

Try to persuade young people not to drink heavily just because other people do. It won't make them look big; they will look just the opposite if they have too much – and they'll feel terrible the next day.

They may also do things you and they wish they hadn't when they've been drinking alcohol.

This could be another topic for discussion.

The following drinks each contain 1 unit of alcohol:

1 single pub measure of spirits | 1 small glass of sherry or fortified wine | 1 small glass of table wine | ½ pint of ordinary lager, beer or cider | ¼ pint of strong lager, beer or cider (Health Education Authority)

As a rough guide a man should not drink more than 21 units a week and a woman no more than 14 units a week.

It's best if young people drink much less than this because alcohol is more likely to be harmful while they are still growing.

If a young person does come home drunk:

- try to keep them quiet so they don't disturb the rest of the house (easier said than done!). They may also be embarrassed the next morning so would prefer as few people as possible to know

- if they want to talk, listen

- if they want a drink, give them water or a cup of tea, sit with them

- if they want to lay down, take them to their room. Wait until they are in bed. Turn them on their side so they don't inhale any vomit. Give them a bowl to be sick into. Before you leave them, let them know they can call you at any time

12. Contraception

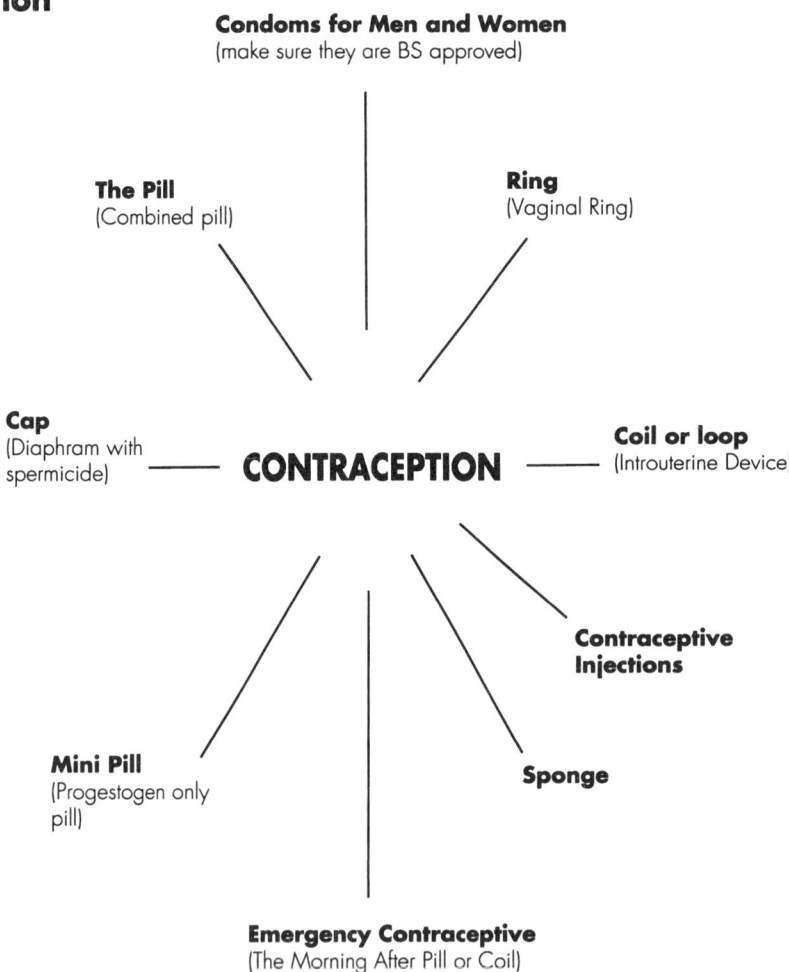

All these are free from

- Youth Advisory Centres
- Family Planning Clinics
- Doctor

Young people can be given advice on the best method(s) for them and on how to use the particular form of contraception.

13. **Suntan** – To many young people having a suntan not only makes them feel good but they think it gives them sex appeal too! It has now been proved that spending too much time in the sun is not a good idea and can cause skin cancer. Here are a few tips:

    - tan slowly – gradually increasing the time spent in the sun each day
    - always use the appropriate sunscreens for different types of skin
    - avoid the midday sun
    - wear a sun hat
    - wear a good pair of sunglasses
    - ABOVE ALL DON'T BURN, tan slowly

    Everyone's skin can burn but people with fair skin, usually those with blond or red hair, are particularly vulnerable.

14. **Preventative Medicine** – The Government has set up Health Promotion Units (often in the telephone book as Health Education) in most towns. The aim is to educate and empower everyone to take control of their lives.

    As well as giving advice on many of the areas mentioned in this section, they also recommend/advise on self-examination of breasts and testicles; they encourage awareness of the possible side-effects of prescribed drugs.

    The diet and lifestyle of young people can have a significant effect on their health in later life.

    Health Promotion staff are happy to talk to anyone; will give lectures; mount displays or provide leaflets.

    Two of their immediate targets are to reduce accidents to young people and to encourage young people to give up smoking.

15. **Advice and Confidentiality** – Sometimes young people find it easier to talk to outsiders about health matters. For free and confidential advice they can go to:

    Their local doctor, the school/college nurse, youth counsellor with responsibility for health, family planning clinics

16. **Medicals** – if a young person is asked to have a medical they have the right to refuse, providing they are of a sufficient age to understand what is going on.

Is it a good idea to keep a record of my health care?

Yes, because:

- later in life they are often asked to fill in forms about their medical records and it will help them to remember details

- they can take their records with them if they move somewhere else

- they may find there is a pattern of regular illness. By looking at their records and thinking what they have done they may be able to work out why

There is a Health Record Sheet on the next page. Young people might like to use it when they are no longer looked after.

It is as well for young people to have a medical check-up and eye test once a year and a dental check up every six months when they become independent. Carers will have guidelines as what is required whilst a young person is being looked after.

Carers must also keep a record of any medicines the young people have taken or must take.

HEALTH RECORD SHEET

Name   **Blood Group**

Name and address of doctor

Telephone number

Visits to the doctor

Treatment	Date

Record of injections

Type of injection	Date

Name and address of dentist

Telephone number

Visits to the dentist

Treatment	Date

Name and address of optician

Telephone number

Visits to the optician

Treatment/advice	Date

DRUG ABUSE

Many young people will have experimented with drugs in some form before they leave school.

Why do they do it?

- it's an alternative to alcohol or solvents

- they like the excitement, the element of danger

- if adults are shocked, that can be an attraction

- they like experimenting with new sensations

- hallucinations/sensations can be interesting and exciting

- hallucinations can also be dangerous, unpleasant and frightening, but even these can be enjoyable (think of horror films)

- drugs allow young people to escape – if only temporarily and only in their imagination

- they may be lonely, feel inadequate, lack self-esteem or confidence and think drug taking will help

- they think it will help them blot out problems

- they are encouraged by their friends or made to look small if they refuse

What to look for

There are often no clear-cut signs and many of the effects are hard to distinguish from normal growing up. Many teenagers are moody without having taken drugs. Look out for:

- sudden change in behaviour or lifestyle, for example, going around with a new set of friends

- wide swings in mood or behaviour – depression, lethargy, followed by being outgoing, active or chatty

- loss of appetite

- being unusually aggressive

- being unusually drowsy or sleepy

- asking for money from their friends or carers without explaining what it is for or with feeble explanations
- loss of money or other objects from the house
- secretiveness or lying
- unusual stains, marks or smells on the body or clothes or around the house

DON'T JUMP TO CONCLUSIONS but be alert to the signs

Watch out also for:

- scorched pieces of tin foil
- a homemade pipe
- the remains of a cannabis cigarette with small cardboard tube filter
- dilated pupils in the eyes
- rash around the mouth

What drugs might they take?

Solvents

Cannabis
(Blo, Grass, Weed)

Stimulants
(Speed, Whizz, Billy, Go fast, Sulph)

Ecstasy
('E', Dove)

Hallucinogens (LSD, acid, magic mushrooms)
(Trips, Tabs)

Tranquillisers

Sedatives

Anabolic Steroids

Heroin
(Methadone, Heroin sub, Smack, Brown, H, Henry)

These have 'street' names which may change with fashion. Some current names are shown in brackets.

Many young people will try taking drugs and stop immediately. Sadly others will not. If they start injecting drugs this can be the most dangerous because of the risks of:

- infection where injecting equipment is unsterile and shared. The most serious infections are HIV (which can develop into AIDS) and hepatitis. If a young person is injecting drugs they may get hepatitis B. Make sure they know the dangers – for example using the wrong injection methods – and get help for the long term but in the short term **make sure they get a supply of clean needles**. (Sometimes these are available free from Drugs Advisory Centres. See pages 167–173.)

- abscesses and thrombosis and other conditions from injecting drugs that were never intended for injection

- gangrene from hitting an artery instead of a vein

- blood poisoning caused by a wound becoming infected

- overdose when a drug of unknown strength is delivered directly into the bloodstream

The question of drug abuse should be discussed at planning meetings or reviews where any decisions will be made

What to do if a young person is 'high'

- keep calm and patient – you have got to try to bring them down

- talk to them about how they feel at the moment

- ask them questions about where they are or what they can see – pink elephants!

- gradually, slowly, quietly explain where they are, who you are

- keep talking, don't threaten, be pleasant – the time for punishments if appropriate and explanations may be later

- sometimes just to leave them to themselves is the best solution but you will need to stay alert

What to do in an emergency

- make sure they've got fresh air
- turn them on their side so they wont choke on their vomit
- don't leave them alone
- get someone to dial 999 and ask for an ambulance
- collect any powders, tablets or anything else that may have been used and give it all to the ambulance driver

How to help prevent drug abuse

- talk to the young people about their views on drugs
- help them have new, interesting and challenging experiences
- get them to think about how they might refuse drugs without losing their friends
- teach them to care for and value their health
- help them build up their self esteem and respect for themselves
- treat them with respect
- take an interest in their opinions and worries
- check out any problems they may have

Where to get advice

At the back of this book there is a list of telephone numbers and addresses of places that may be able to help you or your young persons (pages 167–173).

SOLVENT ABUSE

After smoking and alcohol 'glue sniffing' as it is commonly called, is the most common form of teenage experimentation. Children often start as young as 8-9 years but the peak age is 13-14 years.

They might sniff:

- butane gas (in cigarette lighters and refill canisters)
- aerosol sprays
- correcting fluids (such as Tipp-Ex)
- solvent-based glues (such as Evo-Stik)
- dry-cleaning fluids
- the contents of some types of fire extinguishers
- thinners
- petrol
- liquid shoe polish

Why do they do it?

- its an alternative to alcohol
- they like the excitement, the element of danger
- if adults are shocked, that can be an attraction
- they like experimenting with new sensations
- solvents are cheap and easy to buy or steal!
- hallucinations when sniffing can be interesting and exciting
- they may hate themselves and see the possible self-inflicted damage as a motivator
- hallucinations can also be dangerous, unpleasant and frightening, but even these can be enjoyable (think of horror films). They allow youngsters to escape – if only temporarily and only in their imagination

- they think it will help them blot out problems

- peer pressure

- they may be lonely, feel inadequate, lack self-esteem or confidence

What to look for

There are no clear-cut signs and many of the effects are hard to distinguish from normal growing up. Moodiness may be a result of sniffing but many teenagers are moody without having tried solvents. Look out for:

- finding quantities of empty butane, aerosol or glue cans, or plastic bags in a place where you know young people have been

- chemical smell on clothes or breath

- 'drunken' behaviour

- sudden change in behaviour or lifestyle, for example, going around with a new set of friends

- wide swings in mood or behaviour

- spots around nose and mouth (glue sniffers rash only occurs with some glues and may not be as common as acne!)

- loss of appetite

- asking for money from their friends or carers without explaining what it is for or with feeble explanations

- secretiveness about leisure-time activities

- frequent and persistent headaches, sore throat or runny nose – a quick visit to the doctor would be wise

DON'T JUMP TO CONCLUSIONS but be alert to the signs

A young person told us:

> Solvent abuse is dangerous because the initial "BUZZ" only lasts seconds so a continual use is needed to keep the high going which can lead to suffocation.

How to help

Most young people who try sniffing will only do it a few times and stop without any help from adults. But if you find a young person has tried solvents:

- they may not realise that it's dangerous so telling them of the dangers may be all they need

- don't nag or preach, talk to them, show you are concerned, help them to change their ways

- be a good listener – perhaps there are problems you don't know about. These problems may be far more important than the sniffing

- if they have been sniffing for some time, arrange a health check

- it may be difficult to stop a determined sniffer so stay alert

- arrange other activities together – it will show you care and will give them other things to do. It will also help you to keep track of how they are using their free time

- suggest they join a youth club, take part in physical activities or trips out of town, it'll give them a chance to meet new groups of young people

- for those young people who refuse to stop using solvents you may want to give advice on how to avoid, or reduce damage to their health

Where to get advice or to minimize harm

At the back of this book there is a list of telephone numbers and addresses of places that may be able to help you or your young person (pages 167–173).

HIV/AIDS

HIV is a virus that can get into the blood and destroy the white blood cells leaving the body open to attack from other infections.

AIDS is a condition which develops when the body's defences are not working properly. This means people are more likely to get illnesses which the body would normally be able to fight off easily. These illnesses can be serious or fatal.

At the moment there is no treatment which can cure AIDS.

How is the HIV virus passed on?

- through intimate unprotected (without condom) sexual contact/intercourse between a man and a woman, between men or between women if one of them has the virus

or

- by getting infected blood into their bloodstream when using unsterilised needles or syringes which have been used by an infected person. Drug misusers are especially at risk

  all donated blood used in hospitals is now tested before it is used and blood products are heat treated to reduce the risk of infection

- occasionally women who have the virus can pass it on to their babies during pregnancy, at birth or through breastmilk

You cannot catch the virus by touching objects used by an infected person or by touching an infected person.

Young people will have heard a lot about HIV and AIDS and will often be scared because of what they have heard.

Talk to them openly about sex (page 71) and about drug taking (page 63). If they follow the simple guidelines they will reduce any risk of infection and of catching Aids. Pages 167–173 have telephone numbers a young person may wish to ring to get more information or help.

If a young person is HIV positive or has Aids they will need extra help and support as well as education on just what it all means and how it will affect them.

PERSONAL RELATIONSHIPS AND SEX

Sex should be a normal and healthy part of our lives. As a young person grows up, it is important that they discuss issues about personal relationships and sex with someone they trust. It cannot be assumed that young people have all the necessary facts they need.

What is happening to my body?

Most young people learn the basic 'facts of life' when they are quite young, say 7 or 8. This is usually a very simple explanation given at school. As they reach puberty, young people need to know about periods (page 56), wet dreams, about childbirth as well as about the many physical and emotional changes that occur. Young people in their early teens will have heard all sorts of tales. They may also pretend they know a lot more about sex than they actually do.

Things young people need to know about sex and the law

- it is illegal for anyone (male or female) to have sexual intercourse with a girl who is under 16 years of age. It is illegal for consenting males to have sex with each other until they are both 21 years old

- **rape** – occurs when a man has sex with a woman without her consent. Rape is a very serious offence. The need to give her consent (agree to) is there because a woman has the right to say "No".

  Even when a woman is married if her husband does not obtain her consent to sexual intercourse, this could be an offence of rape

- **indecent exposure** – this is where someone commits an act in a public place which is seen by more than one person and is considered obscene, for example if a man exposes his penis or bare buttocks

- carers whether residential or foster carers cannot have a sexual relationship of any sort with someone for whom they are caring

- the Child Support Act 1991 says that parent(s) have a legal responsibility to financially maintain any babies they have, unless the child is adopted. This applies equally to both parent(s). Absent parent(s) can have deductions taken directly from their wages until that child is 18 years old to pay for the child's keep

What should I think about before I have a sexual relationship?

Nick Fisher from 'Just 17' magazine, writing for the Family Planning Association suggests young people should think about the following before deciding to have sex:

"Do I care for and trust this person very much?"

"Does he or she really care about me?"

"Am I ready to take on the responsibility of a sexual relationship?"

"Will having sex with this person at this time lead to anyone getting hurt?"

"Can my partner and I talk openly and honestly about safer sex and birth control?"

"Is there anything in my culture or religion that says sex outside marriage is wrong?"

"Am I being pressurized into having sex by my partner or friends?"

and **remember**

People often break up with their girl/boy friends quite soon. It is a normal part of growing up and living, but it can be upsetting. That's why having sex before a young person has a long-term relationship and a real commitment can lead to someone getting hurt.

Feeling sexual and wanting to have sex is natural. Deciding to have sex means being responsible and being prepared to handle the consequences.

What if I don't like what is happening to me?

Young people need to know that they have the right to say NO.

No one should force another person to have sex. Everyone's body is their own and they should not be persuaded to do something sexual they do not like; feel unready for or that makes them feel unsafe.

If someone forces another person to have sex, that person is committing a serious criminal offence. If anyone tries to kiss a young person or touches them in a way that worries them, the young person should so NO! and tell someone they trust. The could also phone Childline.

But everybody does it?

Deciding not to have sex with someone is a responsible choice. No one should have sex just because their friends say they do it. Anyway, many young people exaggerate about their relationships. Sex is only enjoyable when both partners feel right about it.

What is safe sex

There is no such thing as "safe sex", only SAFER sex. Apart from the risk of pregnancy, there is the added worry of Aids (page 70). The following are some ways to limit the risks:

- using a BSI approved condom properly to protect one another is an important part of safer sex. It also helps prevent a girl getting pregnant. Condoms can be bought from garages, chemists, machines in toilets, in grocery stores, in fact virtually anywhere. They can be obtained free of charge from local family planning clinics. Condoms are available for women as well as men to use

- limiting the number of partners. The more partners a person has the greater the risk of getting an infection

- not having sex if anyone thinks they, or their partner, has an infection (often you can't tell). Be open and frank about it. If anyone thinks they have a sexually transmitted infection they should straight away go to their doctor or to a special clinic, sometimes called a G-Um or genito-urinary clinic. The address will be in the local telephone directory

- passing urine and washing their sexual parts as soon as possible after sex – this may help prevent passing on an infection

- not having sex if they are drunk. They may either forget to use a condom or not use it properly

What if I get pregnant?

A girl can get pregnant the first time she has sex,

- even before her first period
- even if she has a period at the time
- whatever position is used
- even if she only gets semen near her vagina without having full intercourse at all

When a man and woman have sex they risk starting a baby.

An unplanned baby can totally change the pattern of everyone's lives. That is why young people need to know about contraception (page 58).

Young women also need to know that if they miss a period, or their period is late, this could mean they are pregnant. If they are worried that they may be pregnant they can find out within days of having sex by having a pregnancy test. They can go to their doctor, or buy a pregnancy test kit from the local chemist. Doing the test themselves may not be 100% reliable, especially if they do not follow the instructions carefully.

If a young woman becomes pregnant and wishes to have an abortion she can contact her own doctor, the local health advisory centre or the BPAS (British Pregnancy Advisory Service) which gives confidential advice and counselling. It is very important that she seeks help as soon as possible.

On the other hand, the young woman may wish to keep the baby when it is born. Counselling and practical help will be needed. Many local health authorities have specially trained staff to give this sort of help.

What if I get a girl pregnant?

The man is equally responsible for what has happened. He also has a responsibility to maintain the child until he/she is 18 years of age. Should he not provide adequate maintenance for the child the new Child Support Agency can deduct funds directly from his present and future pay packets.

Am I a lesbian woman or am I gay man?

Young people may have feelings for someone of the same sex. This does not automatically make them lesbian or gay. If it transpires that they are, then they will need positive and non-judgmental support. There are groups/helplines offering help and support for young lesbians and gays, both nationally and locally.

It is officially an offence for gay men to practice sex until they are 21 years old. If you feel you cannot help a young person regarding sexual orientation, there should be well trained counsellors in your area who can help.

Can disabled people have sexual relationships?

Disabled young people have the same feelings and concerns as non-disabled young people. However, they may have a harder time in dealing with them because society often portrays disabled people as non-sexual. Very little information on sexual matters is aimed at disabled people, so it is important they have someone they trust to discuss issues with them.

How do I know this is for real?

Sex, sexuality and relationships are important issues for discussion.

During these discussions, the whole question of relationships can be brought up.

- the value of respecting others and respecting themselves

- not having sex with just anyone because it seems a good idea at the time

- when they meet someone who really means something to them they need to consider carefully whether they are both prepared for the responsibility of having sex

- sex is a lot more complicated than just a matter of feelings. It involves health, happiness and freedom

STAYING WITH FRIENDS

During their time being looked after by social services there often seems to be a lot of niggly little rules and regulations that cause discontent amongst young people.

Staying with friends is one such set of rules.

If you explain the reasons why the rules are there, they may still not like them but at least they will understand.

Can I go to stay with friends?

Yes, of course young people can but you will need to ask where they are going and who they are going to stay with.

You or the young person's social worker will have to find out all you can about the people they want to visit. Parental/guardian permission may be necessary. A police check may also have to be made.

Why do you have to do this?

While young people are being looked after by social services, you must be sure they are safe and well at all times and that there won't be any problems.

Although asking questions about the people they want to visit may be annoying or embarrassing for them, it has to be done to ensure the young person's safety. It also ensures that there won't be people present that the young person is not meant to see.

What happens if I'm baby-sitting and I want to stay overnight?

Whatever the reason for staying out overnight you will need to know in advance. A young person should not stay out overnight until you have found out about the people the young person wants to stay with.

PART TIME JOBS

Can I have a part-time job?

Yes, when they are 13. But they MUST have a **work permit** until they are 16. Some local authorities may do things differently, but the principle is the same.

Why must I have a work permit?

To make sure that:

- a young person is covered by insurance if they have an accident

- their employer obeys the law

How do I get a work permit?

A young person can get a form from their new employer, from their school, or from the education office.

What do I do with the form?

The young person should make sure that every part of the form is filled in, and that their employer sends it to the address shown on the form before they start work.

The young person will be sent an employment card which they must keep in case an inspector asks to see it.

What sort of work can and can't I do?

- young people can't start work before 7 in the morning, or work after 7 in the evening

- on school days they can't work for more than two hours a day. They can only work for one hour before school starts

- no person under 16 or who is of compulsory school age can work:

    - in a quarry or a mine

    - in a factory

    - in the transport industry

    - on a building site

- young people can't make house to house collections before they are 16

- young people can't serve alcohol or petrol until they are 18

GROWING UP

Probably the most difficult phase of our lives is our teens.

Do you remember having spots, big feet, developing breasts, having greasy hair, wearing clothes that didn't suit you, blushing, having a crush on a teacher – the list is endless?

The following section covers some of the topics young people being looked after have asked for help with, such as:

> Decision making
> Discipline and Punishment
> Privacy and Confidentiality
> Self Respect/Confidence
> Values
> Listening and being listened to
> Coping with Crisis
> Worries

Provide them with a happy, warm, caring environment where they can talk about worries openly, have their own privacy and a place to entertain their friends and 'those terrible teenage years' will not be so bad after all.

> "It's nice when all the kids and all the staff get together and have discussions"
>
> "I think a good carer is someone who sits down and listens to you… and someone who will follow it through and try to sort out the problem"
>
> "People who actually work in children's homes and do all the dirty work. I think they understand"

The most valuable thing you can give a young person growing up is your TIME. Time to listen, time to talk, time to communicate, time to understand.

Growing up in the nineties is particularly difficult, they'll need all the help and support you can give them.

DECISION MAKING – CHECKLISTS

Few people like making decisions. We all know it's much easier to put off making decisions until tomorrow! But decision making is an important life skill so young people need help in learning how to make decisions.

They also need to learn decision making so that when they are no longer being looked after, making decisions will be a natural thing to do. Hopefully young people won't rush into things but look at the situation from every angle, exploring the options and then decide.

> "There is pressure on children to make decisions they are not equipped to make" – foster carer

Let them start with simple decisions at first like choosing menus, helping choose holidays, outings, subjects at school, colour schemes, even if it is much easier for you to make the decisions yourself.

The following are 3 ways that could be used to help the decision making process. You could work through them with the young people on a few minor issues at first. You could use them either with just one young person or working in a group.

1 Simple logical method

DEFINE the problem –

what is the real problem?
what is the cause?
what am I trying to achieve?

COLLECT the evidence –

facts and figures
judgments and observations
other people's opinions

GENERATE ideas –

look at the problem from different angles
find all the alternatives

PLAN –

what freedom have I got?
what is the best thing to do for now?
what is the best thing to do for the future?
how will it affect other people?

ACT –

carry out what you have decided
tell others what you are doing

FOLLOW UP –

check that what happened was what you intended

2 For and Against (Pros and Cons)

Make a list of all the good points and all the bad points of making a decision. It is surprising when you have done this how easy the decision will be. If you have more than one choice then you can compare the fors and against. The following is an example:

CHOICE	FOR	AGAINST
Staying on at same school in 6th form		
Going to local college		
Going to college in next town		

3 Rating

Decision making using rating means that you look at the options and then give each option a value. In this way you can work out what each option really means to you.

1. Write down the option or choices at the top of the columns marked X, Y, Z. More columns can be added if needed.

2. Write down all the points/factors that you want to consider in the column marked REQUIREMENTS. Usually about 10 points.

3. Give the points a mark out of 10 (10 being the most important and 1 the least important). Put these numbers in the column marked RATING (a). No number should be used twice in this column. This will show the overall importance to you of the various points.

4. Give X, Y, Z a mark out of 10 to show how well they meet the REQUIREMENTS. Write the mark in column (b). This will show the difference between each option.

5. Multiply the figure in column (a) by the figure in column (b) and put your answer in column (c). Do this for each option.

6. Add up all the scores in each column (c). The highest score will be the best option.

The following is an example of a completed rating form. On the next page is a blank one which can be photocopied and used again and again:

DECISION MAKING FORM

All answers out of 10	RATING	Option/Choice					
		X Staying on at same school in 6th Form		Y Going to local college		Z Going to college in next town	
REQUIREMENTS the things I want	(a)	(b)	(c)	(b)	(c)	(b)	(c)
Choice of subjects	10	7	70	9	90	8	80
Travelling time	4	8	32	5	20	3	12
Travel costs	9	9	81	4	36	8	72
Having friends there	5	10	50	2	10	10	50
Good Pass rate in exams	8	6	48	8	64	9	72
Good sports facilities	6	10	60	6	36	10	60
Library	2	2	4	3	6	4	8
Good social life	7	3	21	5	35	7	49
Nearness to shops	1	1	1	1	1	3	3
Good canteen	3	1	3	3	9	8	24
TOTAL			370		307		430

Ref. No: G&R V4 p105-108, V3 p95-98

DECISION MAKING FORM

All answers out of 10 REQUIREMENTS the things I want	RATING	Option/Choice X		Y		Z	
	(a)	(b)	(c)	(b)	(c)	(b)	(c)

Of course, it may be that once you start putting a value on the requirements they seem less important and you will want to change them.

ENCOURAGING POSITIVE BEHAVIOUR

Behaviour is a way of communicating. With some young people being difficult may be their way, often their only way, of telling you that they feel awful/angry/distressed about something or everything. Extreme behaviour is often related to extreme distress.

When a young person has been particularly difficult, especially if this behaviour comes out of the blue, try to find out what is bothering them – not, of course, until they have calmed down. If the young person is reluctant to talk, you might find the Worries (page 98) helpful.

It is a good idea to make a note of when difficult behaviour occurs to see if there is a pattern. For example, a young person may be 'high' say every Tuesday, after school (they hate the teacher of a particular subject). Someone else may be difficult after reviews or visits home. You can then make your own plans of how to prevent problems occurring.

It is also worth noting when they are not being difficult. You can then speak to them positively and look for ways of lessening the difficult behaviour.

This sort of analysis is called the ABC analysis.

A   Antecedent – what happens before the behaviour

B   Behaviour – what actually happens

C   Consequence – what happens as a result of the behaviour

It is equally useful for positive behaviour as well as for difficult behaviour as it helps build up a picture of the young person's behaviour patterns and will help you to take action accordingly.

How do I know what I can and can't do?

Young people should be encouraged to discuss:

- their behaviour and others' behaviour

- right and wrong

- what is acceptable and what is not

- what control is needed and why

- what sanctions should be imposed, how and by whom. They need to believe the system in their home is fair and is applied across the board consistently

Ref. No: G&R V4 p15-19 (and later guidance), V3 p27

- their relationship with carers, teachers and other young people and why they might feel aggressive towards them; frightened of them; impressed by them

- they need to learn to aim for standards they can achieve

- they need help to find ways to channel their energy and aggression such as taking up a sport, riding their bike or just going for a walk

It is important that the young person learns to be responsible for their own behaviour

I want discipline

"At my review I got what I wanted..I had got used to discipline..and there wasn't any. I asked to be disciplined. My brother asked to be disciplined" – Hampshire teenager.

Young people really do want discipline. They want to know their carers care. They want to know how far they can go and what the consequences will be if they go beyond the boundaries.

In many local authority areas the term care and control is used instead of discipline and punishment but the young people seem to prefer the terms they know.

What is the official guidance?

The following forms of punishment are not allowed in children's homes:

- corporal (physical punishment)

- withholding food, drink and medicines

- restricting contact with family or social workers

- forcing young people to wear clothing that is different or unsuitable

- depriving young people of sleep

- withholding medical or dental treatment

- fines

With regard to punishment, foster carers are given similar powers as parent(s) under the law. They are permitted to enforce "reasonable" discipline and punishment but they should take the above as guidelines.

A good carer will be aware of what is going on in the home and will often be able to diffuse a situation just by being in the room, or in a doorway or in the garden.

However, if a situation gets out of control or the young person is likely to harm themselves or others, then carers may, in exceptional circumstances, use minimum physical constraint or lock doors to prevent escape.

Bedroom doors should not be locked at night although occasionally it may be necessary for the carer to be near the bedroom to ensure the young person does not run away.

A record must be kept if physical restraint is used in residential care.

This sheet has been drawn up using the recommendations for good practice in the Department of Health Guidance on Permissible Forms of Control in Children's Residential Care, April 1993.

The following are some tips that might help you with care and control:

- praise positive behaviour

- work hard to build up a good relationship with the young person

- provide them with a good environment, a home they value. If the place looks good, and the young people are involved in setting the rules and in decisions that affect the home they will behave much better

- involve them in tasks and help them complete these tasks but make sure the tasks are not too difficult and they understand what is required. When the going gets tough some young people may give up. Help them to see the task through, you'll be surprised how pleased they will be. They'll have a sense of achievement even with the most simple task

- find ways to relieve boredom. Look for ways to stimulate young people

- don't say NO too often but if you do say no, then keep to it

- be friendly with the young person. However, they may need to have someone to rebel against and that person will probably be you

- young people will need to learn to trust you and to know you will trust them. They want to respect you – their behaviour may not always indicate this. Be patient

- try to stay one step ahead of the young person. Plan activities, events, discussions

- be ready for possible explosive situations

- be around the house, be available for a chat. It's often just as easy for you to carry out tasks away from the kitchen or office

- TALKING AND LISTENING IS THE REAL KEY TO CARE AND CONTROL

Ref. No: G&R V4 p15-19 (and later guidance), V3 p27

If the young person is very angry or aggressive then:

- don't have a slanging match
- don't swear
- think about what you say
- don't shout
- don't stand in an aggressive way
- let them be angry. Channel that anger. Let them hit their pillow or whack the mattress. You could even give them a rolled up newspaper to do it!
- if they really are aggressive try to move them to another room for their own safety if necessary
- STAY CALM AT ALL COSTS
- wait for the right moment, perhaps when the young person has calmed down to talk to them
- let them know you care

Later, carry out an ABC analysis. It may be something you could do together.

PRIVACY/CONFIDENTIALITY

As young people grow up they have a wish for secrecy; a desire for privacy and confidentiality. Many parent(s) and carers find this difficult to cope with.

This is a very natural part of growing up and should be respected. Young people being looked after hate the thought that they are talked about or that what they think they have told someone in confidence is being passed to someone else. They also hate to think that their file can easily be read by others.

We all want our privacy to be respected and young people are no different:

- letters addressed to them should not be opened or read

- the telephone should be put somewhere so that confidential calls can be taken

- friends should be able to come to visit and be seen in private

- they should have cupboards that can be locked so they can store their own belongings safely

Carers and parent(s) alike are no different and like to see things tidy. Yet young people need their own space where they can leave things as they wish knowing they wont be gone through or examined.

Sometimes if you were to go through a young person's belongings you might find drawings, writings or pictures you wished you hadn't seen or that will shock you. Usually this is just a normal part of growing up, finding out about their sexuality or expressing their feelings and emotions. They would possibly rather die than think someone had seen them.

Young people need to know under what circumstances their 'space' will be entered, e.g. if it is felt the young person is at risk or to clear up the room if it is a health hazard.

Carers will also have their own personal belongings – respecting privacy should be a two-way process. Privacy/Confidentiality can be a good area for discussion

> Some secrets cannot be kept – if you are worried that a young person has suffered or is likely to suffer "significant harm", you may have to take the matter further, but the young person needs to know what you intend doing; why; and to be kept informed.

SELF RESPECT/SELF ESTEEM/CONFIDENCE

> The teacher said "You are a 'no hoper'. You'll leave school with nothing"...she's now at college.

Everyone needs to be valued, to feel special, to feel important. By treating young people looked after as individuals, working and caring for them you will build up their self confidence.

By making opportunities for young people to succeed you will build up their self esteem.

No matter what difficulties a young person has had in the past, they need to know that you expect them to overcome these difficulties. That they are responsible for their own life and behaviour.

Treat them with respect and gradually they will learn to respect you and others around, and also to respect themselves for what they are.

On the next page is an exercise called Know Yourself. Young people might like to do this on their own, with you or in a group. It may help them to look at things with 'fresh eyes'.

To have self respect and to build up confidence they have to understand and know themselves, what makes them tick and realise that they must take responsibility for their own actions.

What other questions might help them do this?

If young people show you their answers, you may be surprised, indignant or hurt but at least you may know the young person a little better.

It could also be used as a talking tool.

KNOW YOURSELF – CHECKLIST
THE 5-POINTER

Write Down:

5 things you are good at:

5 things you are not so good at:

5 ways you could improve:

5 likes/hates:

in food?

in clothes?

at school/college/work?

other things you like/hate

What would make you change any of these answers?

The 5 best points about yourself:

The 5 worst points about yourself:

5 ways you could improve on your worst points:

What do you dislike most about other people?

If it annoys you to answer these 'stupid' questions, think about why

VALUES

The Children Act was introduced to ensure that young people were helped in all sorts of ways so that they learn to become responsible caring adults. Government advisers of the National Curriculum in schools have now issued a set of guidelines stating that teachers should work in PARTNERSHIP with parent(s)/carers to see that young people are able to make responsible decisions in their lives.

Young people want this too. "I want to know right from wrong" said a Hampshire teenager.

They should learn to:

- know the difference between right and wrong
- tell the truth
- keep promises
- respect the rights and properties of others
- act considerately
- help those less fortunate and weaker than themselves
- take personal responsibility for their actions and self-discipline

What does all this mean? It means that you, as the carer of young people, will need to work with them, to help them develop their own sense of values.

They should also be taught to reject:

bullying   cheating   deceit   cruelty   prejudice   discrimination   sexism

Many young people complain if someone cheats on them yet a little later will cheat on others. They need to learn about standards, about what is acceptable and what is not acceptable, and to think about how others feel and not just think about themselves.

As they grow up they will become aware of issues such as:

*damage to the environment   drinking alcohol   smoking   bloodsports   divorce
abortion   loyalty   sexuality*

Group discussions, individual discussions, reading newspapers and watching particular television programmes are all ways that can develop a young person's beliefs.

Of course, young people will always question why things are as they are and will test the boundaries, but there needs to be boundaries so they know where they stand, so they have something to rebel against and so that they have something to stand them in good stead for the future.

Ref. No: G&R V4 p105-108, V3 p97-98

LISTENING AND BEING LISTENED TO

A good communicator should not lie or build up false hopes. They should be trustworthy; reliable and honest and most especially, a good listener.

You cannot listen to young people all the time but you can often spot those who have something important to say by a change of behaviour or mood.

Some simple listening rules

1. Never be too busy to listen. Young people have important things to say at the most inconvenient time of the day.

2. Listen to what is being said. Give the young person your entire attention.

3. Don't anticipate what will be said next. Wait and listen. That way you'll be sure.

4. Keep your thoughts to yourself as to what is being said. Don't let your mind jump away from the topic.

5. Pay attention to both what is being said and 'how it is being said'.

6. If you have a question, make a note of it and ask it at the proper time. Don't interrupt or write while the young person is talking. Asking questions can certainly help but they require careful handling and good timing.

7. If you disagree, don't get angry. Wait until after he/she is finished. He/she may say something that makes your anger unnecessary or even embarrassing.

8. If the young person is continuing for a long time, jot down a few notes. This will help later on in remembering what was said.

   LISTENING IS AS MUCH AN ART AS SPEAKING

   BOTH REQUIRE PRACTICE

   BOTH REQUIRE ATTENTION

A good listener will usually be listened to because they will have taken care to listen and will have thought about what they want to say.

If you want to talk to a young person:

- plan the time and place to suit both of you and if necessary/possible, tell them in advance. Don't choose a time when their favourite TV programme is on!

- plan what you want to say

- jot down the main points you want to say

- have a pen and paper ready to make notes

- tell them at the start what you want to discuss

- end by saying what is agreed and what action is to be taken

- DON'T GOSSIP or pass on what you have heard

- show you are listening by your eye contact, nodding or use of body language

Respect confidentiality/privacy unless you feel the young person is at risk of significant harm.

If you feel you must pass on something you have been told:

- tell the young person, explaining the reasons WHY

- what you will do

- how

- why you are taking that particular course of action

- when you will be doing so

- **at all times help keep them informed of what is happening. Be honest and never make promises you can't keep**

MAKING AND KEEPING FRIENDS

"I'm 17 going on 40"

What Steve went on to explain was that what he had been through in his life up to the age of 17 was probably as much as many people go through up to the age of 40.

"I have nothing in common with anyone who has not been in care"

Again, what he was saying was that he felt that most 17 year olds had very little else to think about other than clothes, parties and discos whereas he had to think about rent, bills, food, budgeting etc, etc as well.

If a teenager has been sexually abused, their sexual awareness may be heightened or the reverse and they may feel revulsion towards that person or anyone else who reminds them of that person. This often makes it more difficult for young people who have been abused to make or trust new friends.

Young people looked after may also have come from difficult backgrounds where they've moved around a lot and not had a chance to make 'best friends'. They may not, therefore, have gone through the usual process of making and keeping friends.

They may also be very lonely so if someone from the opposite sex comes along and gives them some attention they may fall madly in love with them, sometimes to the exclusion of everyone and everything else. This person may also be much older than they are; mother/father figure; car owner; someone with plenty of money. Young people who are being looked after may also not have had a loving caring relationship with an adult.

How can I make new friends?

- young people can be encouraged to have wide interests so they will meet all sorts of people – easier said than done, especially when they are in their early teens. Black young people living with white carers may need help to link up with the black community

- by helping young people to build up their self respect and confidence (page 88)

- by helping young people to understand themselves better, realizing that not only is there probably a good reason why they behave in a certain way but also why other people behave the way they do

- one of the hardest lessons to learn is self-control – not to lose their temper, to count to 10, to try to look at things from others' points of view, not just their own. The best way to learn is by example

- if a relationship is worth having then it's worth keeping; that sometimes you have to compromise; make allowances; or swallow your pride and say SORRY – this goes for adults and young people

- if in your home young people are used to discussing and talking about all sorts of things and listening to others' points of view this will help them with their friendships

One very big problem young people who are looked after find is:

- moving from a family into group living

- moving from group living into:
    - living in a family
    - living on their own
    - living with chosen friends

If they move into a children's home they often give up their friends and are only friendly with those in the home. This a real problem when they move out.

- encourage them to keep their existing friends and also to make new friends outside the home

- if it is possible, get them to stay at their friend's house and to go on school/college trips which entail overnight stays

A new resident in a children's home may find it difficult to cope with the lack of personal attention, the noise, people constantly being around. On the other hand, children's home residents often find the move back home or into foster care difficult to cope with and the closeness hard to handle.

- both groups will need help to handle this change

The loneliness of living independently is also very hard to cope with for a young person who is used to having people around them all the time and someone to call on in time of need.

- make sure they know of all the different points of contact available to help them

COPING WITH CRISIS

We are all different and all have our different ways of coping with crisis. Some young people will wail and cry so you'll know they have a problem, others will bottle it up. Their unhappiness may show up with health problems such as:

physical symptoms

- feeling their heart is beating quickly
- pains and tightness in their chest
- indigestion and wind
- colicky stomach pains and diarrhoea
- frequent passing of urine
- tingling feelings in the arms and legs
- muscle tension, often pain in the neck or low part of the back
- persistent headaches
- migraine
- skin rashes
- difficulty focusing the eyes
- lack of self care/poor hygiene

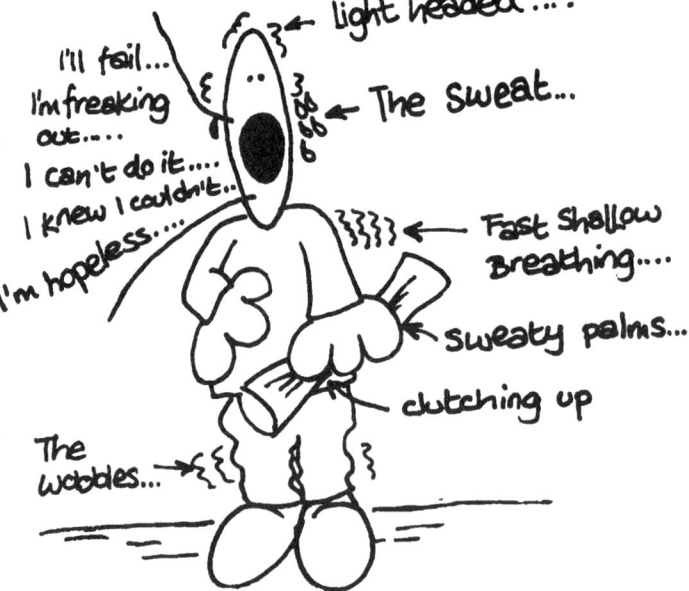

psychological symptoms

- unreasonable complaints
- withdrawal and daydreams
- missing school/college
- accident-proneness and carelessness
- poor work, cheating and evasion
- starting smoking
- drinking alcohol
- trying out drugs
- over-eating or loss of appetite
- difficulty getting to sleep and waking up tired
- feelings of tiredness and lack of concentration
- irritability

Unfortunately many of these may be just normal growing-up symptoms but if they persist then you may find the young person has a problem.

Some tips to help them cope:

- let them know you care
- be available
- be a good listener
- re-assure them
- suggest positive steps such as:
    - talking to their friend, teacher or relative
    - taking part in a physical activity
    - giving themselves a treat
- make them feel secure
- help them become independent
- help them to look at things from all sides
- get them to have a medical check-up. Many problems vanish when they find they've nothing physically wrong with them
- if it's an emotional crisis, help them to cry
- have somewhere private so they can talk or cry without being heard or interrupted

WORRIES

"A friend of mine has a problem....." OR

"I know someone who....."

If a young person starts a conversation like that, that someone is often THEM!

All the time they can talk as someone else they won't get emotionally involved, they don't have to admit they have a problem and also they can go away and think about what you say without feeling under pressure.

Follow up quite soon by asking "what happened?" or "has your friend?" You'll usually be told the truth then. If the matter is serious, get someone else to approach them if you feel you can't get any further or suggest they get in touch with someone from the organisations mentioned at the back of this book (pages 167–173).

We are all different and respond to people differently. Don't be upset if your young person tells their worries to someone else. Very few children are completely open with their own parent(s), preferring to talk to someone less closely involved with them, be it brother/sister, gran, neighbours, friend or teacher.

Something you and most of the world think is unimportant may be really distressing to a sensitive young person:

- be aware
- be concerned
- be patient
- be available

- be tolerant
- be understanding
- be honest
- be discreet

On the next page is a list of problems many teenagers said had worried them at some stage. Young people may like to go through the list and put a tick which says how they feel about things at the moment.

They can, of course, do this questionnaire in confidence, but if they share it with you you'll get a pretty good idea how you can help.

Either way, talking and listening is the best tool for relieving worries.

We all know that even the slightest worry can build up out of all proportion.

A minor illness can be blown up to seem like a major life-threatening disease if there is no one on hand to share that worry with. One young lad, who became aggressive and whose school work was suffering, admitted that he thought he had cancer of the testicles. A quick visit to the doctor soon put his mind at rest

Writing down their worries, both the facts, the situation as they see it and what can be done about it will often help. If they do it with you, you can share their worries and help them overcome them.

If they can't talk to you, suggest other people who might help – teacher, social worker, relative, friend.

Talking really is the best tool to relieve worries.

NOTES

WORRIES – CHECKLIST

Here is a list of other teenagers worries.

	This is a problem for me at the moment		
	Yes	Sometimes	No
Having to go everywhere with adults	____	____	____
The neighbours are too nosey, they talk about me	____	____	____
I feel there are too many people bullying me	____	____	____
I worry about not having enough skills to earn my living	____	____	____
Thinking that nobody will fancy me	____	____	____
People my age not liking me	____	____	____
I don't know what I can do when I go to work	____	____	____
I may fail my exams	____	____	____
I feel all mixed up about life	____	____	____
I have no one to help me with my troubles	____	____	____
I worry friends might turn against me	____	____	____
Not as clever as I would like to be	____	____	____
Is there any point in living?	____	____	____
Too many arguments	____	____	____
Grown ups always complaining about me	____	____	____
Having to go to court	____	____	____
Staying off school/college/work too much	____	____	____
Teachers/tutors not minding their own business	____	____	____
My body is not well developed	____	____	____
I may get pregnant/or get someone else pregnant	____	____	____
Having to be at home by a certain time	____	____	____
Wondering why people aren't nicer to me	____	____	____
Will I be able to do my job well?	____	____	____
People talking about me behind my back	____	____	____
Having no privacy	____	____	____
I might be going mad	____	____	____
Not strong enough	____	____	____
I'm too fat	____	____	____

continued over

Worries Continued – Sheet 2

This is a problem for me at the moment

	Yes	Sometimes	No
Not feeling very clean			
Being bored at school/college			
Not being allowed to pick my own friends			
Being "in-care" – what do people think?			
What shall I tell them?			
I might not get a job			
Nobody seems to understand me			
Not being trusted			
Telling lies			
I am not allowed to go places where I enjoy myself			
Having to wear school uniform or out-dated clothes			
Tough kids always picking on me			
I need advice about which subjects to take for exams			
Wondering if I will know when I am in love			
Making a fool of myself in front of friends			
Do people think I've done something wrong because I'm "in-care"?			
Thinking there won't be any jobs			
Not good at sport			
Being told off too much			
Having too many headaches			
I am not looking good			
Not getting a chance to say what I mean			
Having to keep secrets			
I am not sleeping well			
Being picked on by teachers/tutors			
I am not able to talk to adults			
Not being allowed to bring certain friends back			
Having too many accidents happening to me			
Getting the blame for things I haven't done			
Not knowing what to say when out with people			
No one cares			

Adapted from the PORTEOUS CHECKLIST © Murray A Porteus 1985 by permission of the publishers NFER-NELSON, Darville House, 2 Oxford Road East, Windsor SL4 1DF. All rights reserved.

IDENTIFYING ABUSE

Young people who are looked after may have been abused in one form or another at some time in their life. Sadly, this may also occur during their time 'being looked after'.

What is abuse?

The main forms of abuse are:

Physical abuse: where young people are physically hurt, injured, given poisonous substances and/or drugs

90% of young people who are physically abused have visible injuries, for example bruises in places that do not normally get bruised by accident; and/or bruises of different ages; marks from beating; black eyes; burns and/or scalds, unexplained fractures and head injuries.

Physical abuse should be suspected where the explanation of the injury does not fit the facts, or if the young person is reluctant to say how the injury happened.

Sexual abuse: where young people are exploited by others to meet their own sexual needs. This may be sexual intercourse, fondling, masturbation, oral sex, anal intercourse and exposure to pornographic material including videos.

Common signs of sexual abuse are:

- injuries or soreness in sexual areas and/or mouth
- a wide range of emotional problems (see list on the next page)
- inappropriate sexual behaviour – overly sexual or extreme fear of intimate contact
- knowledge and understanding of sexual matters beyond their age

When it is suspected a young person has been a victim of sexual abuse, they may be interviewed at a special safe place by trained staff, one of whom may be from the police. A video or tape recording may be made of this interview, so the young person doesn't have to keep repeating their experiences.

The young person may be asked to have a medical but they may refuse providing the young person has sufficient understanding to make an informed choice.

Neglect: where young people's basic needs are not met such as food, warmth, medical care, shelter.

Emotional abuse: where young people suffer as a result of a constant lack of affection, verbal attacks, bullying, racial and other harassments, which undermine a young person's confidence and self-esteem.

What are the other signs of abuse?

Any of the following may be associated with abuse and/or may be symptoms of distress:

- poor or deteriorating school/college work/work
- erratic attendance, at school/college/work
- young person's reluctance to go to school/college/work or frequent early morning minor illnesses
- problems with sleeping, nightmares
- complaints of hunger, lack of energy, apathy
- possessions often 'lost', dirtied, destroyed
- desire to stay around adults or avoid adults
- reluctance to attend medicals
- unhappy, withdrawn or isolated
- a new tendency to stammer
- lack of appetite, anorexia, bulimia, excessive 'comfort eating'
- aggression
- constant attention seeking, over-pleasing/compliant behaviour
- indications of alcohol, drug or substance abuse
- attempted suicide
- running away from home
- low self-esteem

Finally

Unlikely excuses to explain any of the above, or refusing to give any reasons for the above.

What are the effects?

Physical scars heal but many young people take longer to recover from the emotional trauma of physical and sexual abuse. They may need professional help.

Young people who have been sexually abused over a long period of time may have little understanding of what is appropriate sexual behaviour. This will have to be learnt. Carers must be aware of this and ensure that they do not place themselves in situations which could be misinterpreted.

What happens if a carer suspects abuse?

Where carers are concerned that a child has been abused, they should record their concern, share their concern with a senior staff member and consult their child protection manual. In some cases they may have to speak to someone outside their own organisation.

Breaking confidentiality is a big problem as some young people will tell you, begging you not to tell anyone else. If you have evidence that a young person is being abused then you must pass this on. You will have to explain this to the young person. They'll hate you at first but will be relieved when they know that something is being done. Keep them informed.

How can carers help young people who may have been abused?

Carers can help by:

- listening to what a young person says
- avoiding asking too many questions or asking for unnecessary detail
- being alert and observant
- protecting the young person
- trying to find out what a young person is afraid of
- where a young person is in danger of serious harm, carers must follow the procedures for protecting the young person
- telling the young person what you are going to do and what will happen next
- never telling lies to the young person

Who are the abusers?

Most young people who have been abused are abused by those they know and even like – older friends, parent(s), relatives, carers, neighbours.

This is particularly difficult for the young person to cope with as they do not want to cause a problem to those close to them but that person may go on to abuse others. You will have to help young people to understand that what abusers do is wrong, that the young person is not to blame, but that everyone must be protected from the abuser.

What are a young person's rights?

Young people are entitled to be protected from all forms of abuse

- let them know they are not alone and that you are there to protect them
- many young people will find it hard to talk about being abused
- they need to know that you can be trusted
- they need to know that you will believe them
- they need to know they are not to blame
- but they need to know that some 'secrets' cannot be kept

Check your local Child Protection Procedures for further details.

BULLYING

Many young people suffer really badly because they are bullied. Young people who are bullied are entitled to be protected. They often don't tell anyone in case they are thought of as 'grassers'.

Many of the effects of abuse mentioned on pages 103–106 may apply to a young person who is being bullied so carers need to be observant. Studies show that over half of all young people say that have been bullied at some time.

What can I do if I am being bullied?

'Who Cares?' magazine makes the following suggestions for young people who have been bullied. You may like to pass these on or use them as a basis for discussion.

- suggest the young person gets help, talks to someone they can trust such as their social worker, carer or someone at school

- if they are worried that telling will make matters worse, let them know that you will be discreet

- if it doesn't get sorted straight away, tell them not to give up. Many schools/colleges have an 'anti-bullying' policy so schools/colleges need to know what is going on

What else can I do?

The following are 5 useful tips that might also help a young person:

1. Don't let bullies think they are scaring you. Try to ignore or laugh at what they say – it's hard but worth a go.

2. If you do get angry and realise it would have been better staying calm, don't let it show. Walk away as soon as you can.

3. Stay with a crowd – bullies usually pick on you when you're on your own.

4. Keep a diary. Write down what happens each time you are bullied, what is said, when and where. Give this information to those who are helping you.

5. Take up self defence! This doesn't mean 'fighting back', but it will make you feel more confident. Ask about self defence classes where you live.

NO ONE SHOULD TOLERATE BULLYING

CARERS NEED TO MAKE IT CLEAR THAT BULLIES HAVE NO PLACE IN THEIR HOME.

LOSS & BEREAVEMENT

Young people may react to divorce or separation by their parents in a similar way to someone dying. Our society finds it difficult to talk about death so we have focused on bereavement.

On hearing the news of the loss of someone they know and love they will feel a sense of shock and disbelief. A numbness.

This may be followed by:

- misery
- anger
- questioning
- sadness
- self-blame
- blaming others

If a young person knows in advance that the loss is to occur they will have time to prepare themselves mentally. The impact of the loss is much greater if the loss is sudden.

Different young people react to death in different ways. They may:

- cry
- go for long walks alone
- hide in a crowd
- be angry
- eat too much or too little
- smoke or drink alcohol to excess

Let them find their own way. When the time is right, talk to them or let them talk to you:

- talking helps to dispel wrong ideas

- talking helps to make good sense of the loss

- talking helps to lift the burden of responsibility that many young people will feel. For example if there was a car crash and they survived and their mother didn't, they would feel guilt. If they were out enjoying themselves at a party when their father died they will say "if only..."

    Sometimes this burden may be realistic and they will need help to come to terms with this

Young people will feel pain, let them. Don't try to get them to get over it too quickly. There is no set time that bereavement lasts.

They will feel desolation and despair. They will feel there is no sweetness, no purpose, no point in their lives –

"Who am I?"   "What does it mean for me?"   "I'm an orphan"

may be said many times.

The pain will recur again and again – at birthdays; anniversaries; at Christmas; at holiday times and at other times that were special for the particular family.

There are times in their life when the loss may be re-experienced such as weddings, the birth of their child, leaving school.

Life moves on and the young person will adapt and adjust but bereavement is never fully dealt with.

Help them find practical things they can do, such as collecting mementos or photographs or writing down how they feel.

A YOUNG PERSON'S VIEW

Today's care leavers are tomorrows citizens and parent(s).

An 18 year old who had recently left care was asked what she thought should be provided for care leavers.

The following is exactly what she wrote down in no particular order, just as it came to her:

- there should be hostels and flatlets with a live-in warden. Normal renting rules should apply – interview, deposit, contract etc. It should be available to everyone

- THERE SHOULD BE CONSISTENT AFTERCARE ADVICE FOR ALL AND HELP

- there should be drop-in centres at the children's home on certain nights or in an emergency

- there should be a proper meeting before you leave care with your social worker, carer, possibly parent(s) and young person to discuss all the arrangements. This should include an aftercare booklet

- there should be a full back-up system if things don't work out. This should be settled before you leave

- social services should check your living accommodation fully

- moving out should be a gradual process

- plans should be made so that young people who have recently left care and who have nowhere to go, have somewhere they can drop-in for Christmas

- there needs to be a helpline for everyday matters

- a list of people who are willing to listen and give advice, ie education, careers, money, sexual, religion, culture etc

- there should be an emergency 24 hour line for problems – drugs, suicide, sexual, family affairs

- an emergency refuge where they can get you in touch with someone to talk to or a place to stay temporarily

PREPARATION AND PLANNING

The most common worry young people have is "What will happen to me when I am 16 and will no longer be looked after by the local authority?" They see news coverage about homeless young people and worry that it might turn out to be them.

Young people need you to talk about and plan their future with them. **You cannot start too soon**. You are the best person to help them. There is a checklist at the back of this chapter (pages 133–140) that they might like to use.

Young people will need life skills like:

coping with crisis, making and keeping new friends

Young people will need money skills like:

budgeting, saving, filling in social security forms

Young people will need to learn practical skills like:

changing a plug, cooking, cleaning

Other questions they might ask are:

When can I stop being looked after by social services?

- when the young person, their carers, their social worker and those with parental responsibility think they are ready

- if the young person is on a care order, when the court decides the young person no longer needs to be looked after by social services or when they are 18

Can I still contact social services after I become independent?

Yes, social services must give advice and help young people aged 16 – 21 who have been looked after.

Do I have to become independent?

Yes, a time will come when the young person will find it difficult to live by the rules of the children's home or their carer's home.

They will probably want to leave when they reach 18, although some young people start living independently as young as 16.

Will I still be able to go back to visit?

Yes, most children's homes and foster carers will welcome young people back for visits. It may be possible for them to stay overnight.

Some young people find becoming independent a really big problem and need to go back to their previous home. Of course you should welcome them.

Will I get help to prepare for becoming independent?

Yes. A joint plan should be drawn up between the young person, you, their social worker, if they have one, and other interested parties such as their school, the housing department or health authority.

The plan should show:

- what they are going to do when they become independent
- where they are going to live
- what help they will receive
- who will help them
- what happens if things go wrong
- how they will manage financially (page 39)

Everyone involved should be given a copy.

You could also encourage them to join or form a group of other similar young people so they can support each other.

Will I get any money to help me buy what I need?

Social services have a special 'one-off' allowance that should be given. Most young people are entitled to this. Make sure they get what they are entitled to.

If they stay in full-time education they can receive financial support from social services until they are 21 years old.

If after being independent they decide to study they may still be entitled to an allowance. They should ask social services about this.

Normally Citizens Advice Bureaux, Welfare Advice Centres, Housing Associations or the Department of Social Security will tell them of any money they might get. Most telephone numbers will be in the 'phone book. Help them to get as much money as they are entitled to.

The most important thing they will need is re-assurance. It will be a very big step for them:

- arm them with all the facts you can
- help them get all their allowances
- let them know that someone cares
- tell them that there will always be someone to turn to in time of need

The National Foster Care Association, have produced a very useful guide for young people preparing to leave a children's home; foster home; hostel or independent living scheme. It is called 'Stepping Out' and it's FREE. For more details contact NFCA whose address is at the back of the book.

Young people who have been looked after are entitled to support by the local authority after they become independent. They are also entitled to information on what help is available.

Training

Many local authorities are providing training courses to help young people cope with the problems of leaving care. What young people often need most is help in coping with the emotional side of things – that is where you come in!

There are also many courses to help carers prepare young people to become independent.

HOUSING

When a young person is ready to leave care their choice of what sort of place to get will depend largely on where they want to live.

They usually say "I'm going to get a flat" or "stay with friends". Both of these are often much more difficult than they realize.

Although staying with friends can be useful while they are getting themselves sorted out and costs little or no money, it may mean sleeping on the floor, having no privacy and losing their friends if they stay too long! Their friends may also lose any benefits their friends are entitled to as well.

Not only is renting a flat very expensive it can also be very lonely if a young person is on their own.

Where can I live?

Other choices they might think about are:

- go back to live with family or relatives
- find lodgings in someone's house
- share a house or flat with other people
- find a bedsit
- live in a hostel
- find bed and breakfast accommodation but only as a last resort
- supported lodgings if they are available

What should I think about?

Get them to think about:

- the good points and bad points of each
- make a list of what would be their ideal
- another list of what they would accept

then you can go about helping them find a suitable place.

How do I find a place to live?

Local social services departments have under The Children Act a duty to help any young person who has been "in care". This may mean helping them find appropriate accommodation. There may be someone specially appointed for this task or you and the young person can do it together.

Together you could try:

- looking in local papers and adverts in shop windows

- putting an advert in a shop window or at a community centre

- accommodation agencies – they may ask for a deposit and a fee for finding accommodation

- council housing department – they have long waiting lists and may not be able to help until the young person is 18. They may have a list of bed and breakfast accommodation and housing co-operatives and housing associations. Let the housing department know all the relevant information about their particular needs as the local authority may have certain responsibilities to young people who have been looked after

- housing co-operatives provide cheap housing for members. Members sort out rent, choose new members, maintain and repair the accommodation. For more details contact the National Federation of Housing Cooperatives, tel: 071 253 0202

- housing associations manage and sometimes build housing for particular groups of people. They are in close contact with local advice agencies who refer people to them

Make sure a young person gets on the local authority's housing waiting list and stays on it even if it seems hopeless at the time.

HOUSING CHECKLIST

Many local authorities run courses to help young people prepare to leave care and others leave it to their carers to help them.

Either way, a young person could go through the following checklist when they have found somewhere they think is suitable to live.

Accommodation Checklist

Is it near work/college/shop/bank/buses/trains?

Cost £   per month   **Deposit £   Get it back?**
which equals £   cost per week

Pay rent? weekly/monthly

What's included?   **rent/gas/electricity/rates/tv/'phone/other**

Notice to leave by you or landlord?   **weeks/months**

Contract to sign?   **Yes/No**

Have you or someone else read it? Checked it?   **Yes/No**

Rent book?   **Yes/No (get it signed every time you pay rent)**

Inventory (list of what's there)   **Yes/No   Checked correct?   Yes/No**

Does everything work and in condition stated?   **Yes/No**

If not, agree with the landlord who will get it repaired and how the repair is to be paid for.
Don't sign anything until this is done.

Read the meters?   **Yes/No   Agreed with landlord?   Yes/No**

> ** Watch out for high rate meters that use money fast*

GETTING A JOB – A YOUNG PERSON'S CHECKLIST

Some things to think about and some hints for getting a job.

What kind of job do I want?

Do you want:

- a manual job or an office job?
- to work on your own or with other people?
- to work indoors or outdoors?
- a job where you dress smartly or where you can wear casual clothes all the time?

Do you mind:

- taking orders?
- working evenings, weekends or shifts?

How do I find the right job?

- talk to as many different people as you can, not just careers advisers or careers teachers
- use your school careers service. They may have a questionnaire you can fill in to help you to decide. They will also help you to use their library system to choose a suitable job
- don't just think about one type of job but collect information about others that might suit you

When you have some ideas about what you want to do, find out:

- what the job involves
- what qualifications you need
- what qualifications you will get whilst working
- what training you will be given
- what the prospects are for promotion or moving on

How do I find a job?

Careers Offices
One of the best sources of local jobs for young people.

Local Papers
If you can, get hold of the local papers from neighbouring areas as well.

National Papers
Some vacancies for school leavers are advertised in the national press.

Public libraries have copies of many newspapers which can be read every day. It will save buying them and save money.

Job Centres
Many types of jobs are advertised here. If you can't see what you want, ask.

Employment Agencies
If you have work experience or a skill, like typing, agencies may take you on their books.

Personal Contacts
Ask friends and relatives to keep their eyes open and tell you about any suitable vacancies that come up.

When jobs are not easy to find it is especially important you take a lot of care with your applications.

How do I apply for a job?

- if you see an advert in a local or national paper, the advert you see may tell you your next step, which may be to:

    - ring for an application form

    - write for an application form

    - ring saying why you feel you could do the job

    - write saying why you feel you could do the job

    - write saying why you feel you could do the job and enclose a CV (see page 122)

    If in the advertisement it says "**write** for an application form" then it means do **not** telephone. Your letter may however be typed. If it says apply in **your own hand writing** then it MUST NOT be typed.

- you may see a job advertised that you think you would like and could do but do not have the qualifications then:

    - write and tell them about yourself explaining exactly what you have to offer

    - it may be that the qualifications asked for are only a guideline

    - it may be the employer is confused about the different qualifications. This happened recently when a job was advertised asking for 'A' level maths. When the careers teacher telephoned and explained details of 'A' level maths the company soon realised that the job did not call for that level of ability

- if you see a job that you want to apply for advertised in the job centre or in an employment agency, the staff there will either arrange an interview for you or tell you how to apply if they think you are suitable for the job

- if you have to telephone:

    - be prepared to explain why you want the job and what skills you have to offer

    - if you're using a public telephone use a phonecard so that your money doesn't run out in the middle of your call

    - don't hang up if you hear an answering machine – leave your name and details of where you can be contacted

if you have to write:

    - you should say clearly what job you are applying for, where you saw it advertised and ask for an application form

    - give three or four reasons why you should be considered for the job

Here is an example of a job letter:

>
> 16 The Gardens
> Orchard Green
> Southampton
> Hampshire
> S052 3YB
>
> Tel: 0703 000000
>
> 14 February 1999
>
> Ms Fanthorne
> Smith & Company
> 43 Cranbourne Road
> Portsmouth
> Hants
> PO1 ABC
>
> Dear Ms Fanthorne
>
> I wish to apply for the position of Junior Secretary at Smith & Company which I saw advertised in the Fullborough Evening Echo on 13 February. I enclose a copy of my CV.
>
> I would like to be considered for the position because I have gained good grades in my GCSE examinations and wish to put my skills to good use. I am responsible and work well on my own.
>
> I hope to hear from you soon.
>
> Yours sincerely
>
> Ian Jackson

- if you can't find out who to address the letter to, put 'Dear Sir or Madam' and then end your letter 'Yours faithfully'

- you can alter the letter if you are enclosing an application form rather than your CV (see page 122)

- keep the letter neat and avoid spelling mistakes – get someone to check it before you send it off

Here is an application form checklist:

1. Check the closing date and make sure you apply in time.

2. Read instructions carefully. Are you asked to use a black pen? Do you have to use block capitals on any part of the form?

3. Your application form will be the first impression the employers will have of you. It must be neat and well presented or it will be filed in the bin!

4. If you only have one copy of the application form, work out your answers on rough paper first, then fill in the form in light pencil before filling it in with a pen. If you can, photocopy the blank form and practise first.

5. Always give honest answers to all questions. You will probably be asked about your application form when you go for an interview.

6. Get someone to check it (e.g. your carer or a teacher) before you send it.

7. Keep a copy and read it before your interview.

You will be able to use your CV for most of the details.

CV

CV stands for **curriculum vitae**, which is latin for 'the course of your life'. It is a way of recording the most important things about yourself.

Sometimes you are asked to send a CV when you apply for a job.

It will look better if you can get it typed but don't worry if that's not possible. You can get it photocopied as many times as you need.

A CV gives all the basic information an interviewer will want to know about you.

There is a CV example on the next page.

Here is a CV checklist:

1. Write down your name, age, date of birth, address and telephone number.

2. Details of your education and training should come next. List, with dates:

   - your present school/college or any other secondary schools or colleges you've attended
   - the exams you've taken (or are about to take)
   - the exams you've passed, with grades
   - any training with details of other qualifications, awards and achievements e.g. first aid certificate or life saving award
   - any position of responsibility you've held e.g. captain of netball or rugby team, member of the school orchestra

3. Put down all the work experience you've ever had.

   - include holiday work, Saturday jobs, helping relatives or friends in their work or business, and work experience arranged by school/college
   - give brief details about what you did. Don't forget to say how long it was for, and when it was

4. Put down any special skills, spare time interests and hobbies you have, and clubs and societies you belong to.

5. You will need to give names and addresses of two or three people who know you well enough to say how suitable you are for the job. (What they write about you is called a reference.)

- include details of their position or how you know them, (e.g. a teacher at school or college), someone you have worked for (e.g. for a Saturday job) and someone who knows you through a club or group

- ask them if they would be happy to act as referee for you. Make sure that they know each time you apply for a job and what the job is so that they can say why they think you could do it

Here is an example of a CV:

CURRICULUM VITAE

NAME	**AGE**	**DATE OF BIRTH**
Samantha Brooks	15	23rd June 1978

ADDRESS	**TELEPHONE NUMBER**
26 St. John's Avenue Fareham Hampshire PO25 1XX	0123 0000

EDUCATION AND TRAINING

1987-1992: Ballharbour Comprehensive School

I will be taking the following exams in June:

English	GCSE
Mathematics	GCSE
Geography	GCSE
Biology	GCSE
Music	GCSE

I have also gained my bronze life-saving award.

EMPLOYMENT AND WORK EXPERIENCE

I have worked in Newswell newsagents on Saturdays since November 1992.

INTERESTS

I enjoy badminton and swimming and I also help run the school aerobics club.
I am a member of the school choir and I play the piano to grade 3 standard.

REFEREES

Mrs. P. Green Head of School Ballharbour Comprehensive School Smarts Lane Fareham PO23 2YZ Tel: 0123 66666	Mr. S. Singh 42 Station Road Portsmouth PO1 1 ZZ Tel: 070512345 (Manager of Newswell)

When some companies have a vacancy for a job they draw up and send out a person specification highlighting the qualities they are looking for in their employee. If this happens, you may need help with this application to show that you have the particular qualities – you may not think you have or be confident enough to say so – ask your carer to help.

Preparing for your interview:

- find out what you can about the job and the company

- talk over with your social worker or your carer/keyworker why you want the job and what you can offer

- decide in advance what you are going to wear and get it ready. If you aren't sure what to wear, ask your carer. Wear something that is comfortable but smart

- make sure you know exactly where the interview will be and how long it will take you to get there, so that you arrive in good time

- look at the copy you have of your application form to remind yourself of what you have said

- when you arrive say you have come for an interview and ask at the reception desk where you should go. You will be shown where to wait

At the interview:

- be friendly to everyone that you meet from the company

- when you go in, look at the interviewer and shake their hand if they offer their hand to you. A too bold handshake is bad but a wet wishy one is worse! Only sit down when asked

- don't chew gum or smoke, even if offered a cigarette

- sit in a straight and upright (but relaxed) position and don't fidget

- think before you reply and then answer the question fully, not just 'yes' and 'no'

- be alert and interested. Sound positive and enthusiastic

- at the end of the interview, thank the interviewer and say goodbye

Likely questions you might be asked:

- why do you want to work for us?
- what have you got to offer?
- what were your favourite subjects at school?
- what are your long-term aims?

At the end of the interview you may be asked if you have any questions, so prepare some in advance. If you can't think of anything, just say "I think you covered everything I need to know". Before you leave try to find out when you will hear the result.

You may find that there are two people to interview you at the same time; speak to whoever asks you the question.

After the interview you might:

- get a job offer either by phone or in writing

    If you are offered a job and you want to take it, write immediately saying thank you for the offer and how pleased you are to accept it. If you decide not to accept the offer, write back and say so as soon as possible

or
- get asked to come back for another interview

    This may be with the same interviewer or with somebody you have not met before

or
- be told you haven't got the job

    Ask the company why you were not successful. Think about the reasons why you were not chosen and learn from the experience so that you are well prepared for the next interview you get

or
- hear nothing at all

    If you have heard nothing within 2 weeks, telephone and ask whether a decision has been made

Replying to a job offer

When you reply to an offer:

- reply as soon as you can
- follow instructions e.g. telephone if it says to do so
- set out your reply correctly
- write neatly
- cover all the points mentioned

Review Sheet

It's a good idea to keep a record of the job applications you have made.

You could include:

Name of Company
Job title
Date of application
Date reply received
Action
Results
Comments

CAREERS

Local authorities must by law provide a careers advisory service. What is available will vary from area to area. Some authorities provide an extra allowance so that young people looked after can be given special help if they need it.

What do the careers staff do?

The careers centres will welcome both you and your young people and give help and advice not just on what jobs are available but also:

- opportunities in further education
- opportunities in training
- enterprise schemes for young people
- voluntary work
- career preparation and planning
- counselling/vocational guidance

In fact, all kinds of information, support and help for a young person taking the next step in life. They will also have specialist information for black young people. Interpreters may be provided for young people whose first language is not English. Young people with disabilities should also receive special help.

Must I go to their office?

If you work in a children's home someone from the careers service may be willing to come to work with the young people in their own environment.

Whatever the circumstances, find out what is available and try to get your young people to make the best use of it.

WORK

How to get a job and how to keep it!

Helping a young person to choose a job and actually get it requires skill and patience. Although many schools and colleges give very good advice, often a young person will listen to the person closest to them – YOU.

Some young people will think they want to be a hairdresser, a nurse, a footballer or a builder. They will need help to look at all the options.

Many schools/colleges offer young people the chance to take part in a works experience programme. Encourage everyone to take part. **It's as good a way as any to find out what they don't want to do as much as what they do want to do.**

Try also to get them to think of the longer term rather than to think only of the present and of just getting any old job. The money they get now might be good now, but probably won't improve much in the future when they have other commitments.

Many young people think of the government's youth training scheme as slave labour and in a few cases this may be true. But it is not usually the case and it gives an opportunity to learn new skills and obtain qualifications. Discourage them from turning down this option out of hand. Try to get them to think about it first. You could also visit the scheme with the young person.

Some young people feel that to employers there is a stigma of 'being in care'. Prepare them in case they come across this. Give them help and advice on how to handle the situation. Help them to have an answer ready in case they are asked WHY?

Once they've got a job, the important thing is to help them keep it.

When I start work, what do I need to know?

Many of these young people will have lived unsettled lives and the discipline and the stress of going to work will not come easy. Do you remember your first day at work? Talk it through with them and also remind them of such essentials as:

- good time-keeping – not just at the start of the day but after breaks

- attendance – good attendance is a must, but if they really are too ill to go to work, either they should 'phone in or they must get someone else to explain the situation and say when they may be expected back

- asking if they don't understand – no one minds repeating something but they will mind incorrect work

- everyone makes mistakes – tell them to own up promptly and provided mistakes don't happen too often no one will mind too much, particularly for new staff

- they will be the junior and may not be spoken to as they should – this is not right but may happen. Help them to 'bite their tongue' and not react – think first, count to 10

- many jobs, especially in the early days may be boring – don't let them give up:

    - if they stick at it they'll probably be given a better job when one is available

    - they'll actually feel quite pleased with themselves as well. It should give them confidence and self respect

    - it's easier to get another job when they're in a job than if they're unemployed

    - it will be a useful talking point at another interview

    - they'll probably get a reference from their first employer

A young person who has had a disruptive childhood may need to try several jobs before settling into the right one for them. They will need all the help and encouragement you can give them.

What if I think I'm being discriminated against?

At work young people may find they are victims of discrimination. They may need your help to handle this and to know their rights. Discrimination in any form is not acceptable. There are two laws – the Race Discrimination Act 1976 and the Sex Discrimination Act 1975 that can be used as a last resort if all else fails to resolve the problem. At present there is no law governing discrimination on the grounds of sexuality. The Disabled Persons (Employment) Acts 1944 and 1955 state that registered disabled people may get some help with employment.

In most jobs, appearance and personal hygiene are important and many young people find looking clean, tidy and smart all the time difficult. Help them to understand that they are now representing their company and must create the right image. In practical ways help them to make sure they have room to hang their clothes properly, or to wash and iron them. Advise them on the best material to choose for any new clothes they buy or on their make-up, jewellery or hairstyle. The young person's social worker may be involved in some of this work.

Ref. No: G&R V4 p116, V3 p106

FEELING ISOLATED AND LONELY – SUPPORT NETWORKS

If a young person feels isolated or lonely they could contact or visit any of those shown below.

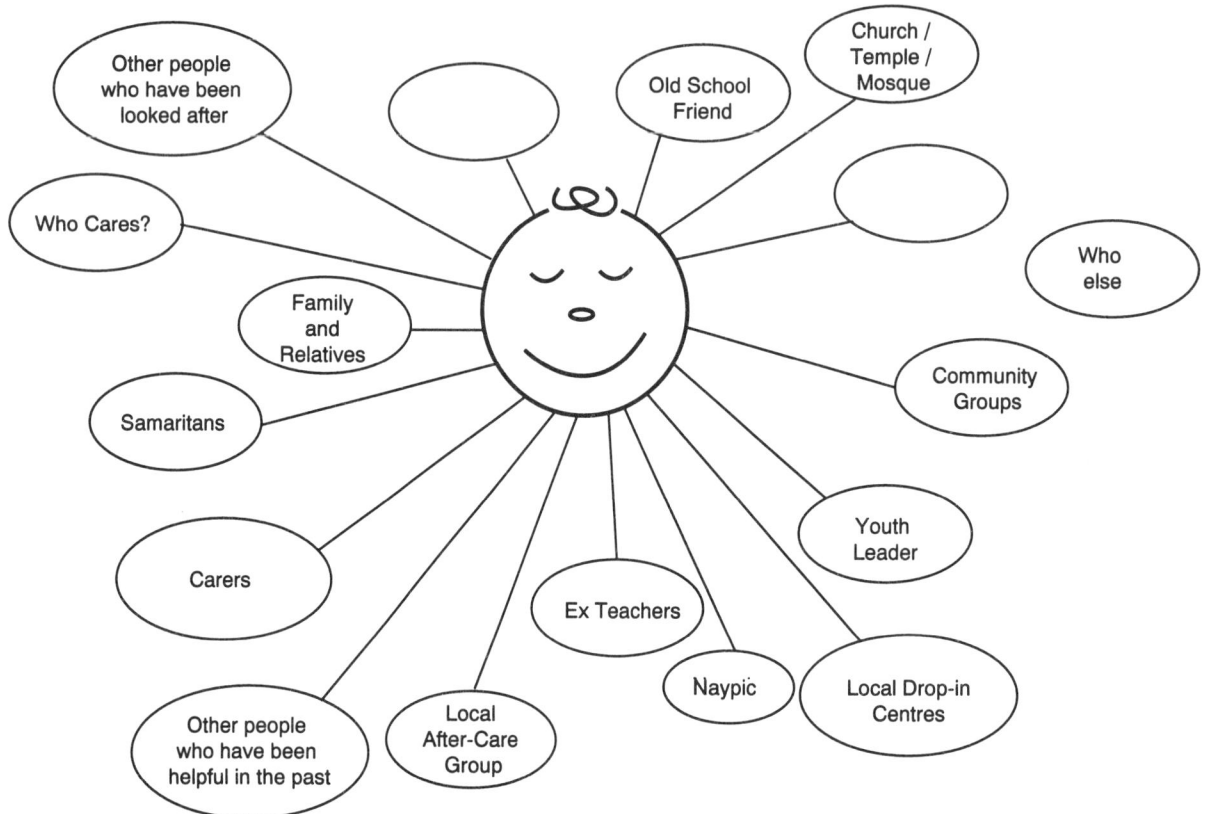

Who else might help?

What practical things would help?

- keep an address book with names, addresses and telephone numbers of families, friends and any of the above

- swap addresses with friends

- let everyone know their new address if they move on

- give an address of someone who will know where the young person is and let other people know who it is. Someone may want to contact them

What else might help?

Taking some positive action like:

- doing something to help others
- going jogging, swimming or doing some other physical activity
- taking up a new hobby or sport
- joining a club or society
- learning a new skill
- changing the layout of a room, spring cleaning it or even decorating it
- drawing their own support chart

BECOMING INDEPENDENT

The aim of the checklist on the next page is to find out what a young person knows and how ready they are for independence.

The questions are not so much 'can' as 'DO' they do this.

The questionnaire can be filled in, in one go, or in stages. They can go back and add or change things whenever they wish. It is NOT a test.

It can be photocopied and used again by the same young person in say a year's time.

The areas covered are:

- helping young people to build relationships with others

- helping young people to develop self-esteem and pride

- practical and financial skills and knowledge

- their future

The checklist also asks what they think, as it is important for young people not just to have knowledge, but to think about getting as much information and help as they can.

- talk over their answers with them

- help them make a plan, with a time-limit, of what help they would like

This checklist could also be used as a way of discussing how other young people could be better helped to prepare for their independence.

INDEPENDENCE CHECKLIST

Name _____

Age/D.O.B. _____

Keyworker _____

Date Completed 1st Time _____

Date Changes Made _____

_____

_____

A. Education or Employment

1. Which of the following are you doing? Circle the answer and state which school/college or workplace.

    a) Local School/College – Full-time/Part-time _____

    b) Further Education – Full-time/Part-time _____

    c) Work Experience, how much?, where? _____

    d) Youth Training, where? _____

    e) Employed – Full-time/Part-time _____

    f) Unemployed/Registered with Careers Office _____

2. Would you say that you attended the above – Regularly/More Than Half/Less Than Half?

    _____

3. Why do you think your attendance is the way you say it is?

    _____

B. Social Contact

1. Do you attend, belong to, take part in one or more of the following?

    a) Church/temple/mosque/synagogue – Regularly/Sometimes _____

    b) Local Youth Club – Regularly/Sometimes _____

    c) Sports Club – Regularly/Sometimes _____

    d) Hobby/Activity – Regularly/Sometimes _____

    e) Outdoor Activity Trips _____

    f) Duke of Edinburgh Award – what level and what activities? _____

    _____

    g) Other _____

2. Is there any other outside event or place that you go to where you meet other people? (e.g. a disco, the town centre)

   _____ How often? _____

3. Do you know of any places where you can get a discount on leisure schemes in your area? (If not, would you like help to find out?)

   _____

4. Do you have friends of your own age locally? Do they visit you, or you them? Have they stayed overnight, at your house, or have you stayed at their place?

   _____

5. Do you have any older friends? Who?

   _____

C. Family

1. Which members of your family are you in touch with? For example: parent(s), brothers and sisters, step-parent(s), foster family. What type of contact – telephone? visits? How often?

   _____

   _____

2. Do you know about your family history?

   _____

3. Would you like to know more? If so what else would you like to know?

   _____

4. Do you know where to get more information?

   _____

5. Is there anyone you would like to contact or trace?

   _____

D. Achievements

1. What school/college qualifications have you got or are expecting to get?

   _____

   _____

2. What sports or hobby awards/certificates have you?

   _____

3. Have you done any other courses or training? (e.g First Aid)

   _____

4. What personal ambition or resolution have you achieved in the last year?

    _____

5. Have you attended any job interviews (including work experience)? Have you been offered a position?

    _____

E. Taking part in Making Decisions About Leaving

1. Do you have group meetings that you go to? _____

2. Do you attend your reviews? (date of last one) _____

3. Which area do you want to live in, when you leave? For example: locally, or near your family if they live in a different area?

    _____

4. Would you choose to, live with – family, friends, foster carers or supported lodgings, in independent living units, or on your own?

    _____

    _____

F. Practical Skills (reading, writing and maths)

1. Do you read a newspaper/magazine? Which one? _____

    (If not, would you like to?) _____

2. Do you understand job adverts in the paper? _____

    (If not would you like help to?) _____

3. Can you write a letter? (e.g: applying for a job) _____

    (If not would you like help to?) _____

4. Have you got a C.V. (personal information sheet) for job applications? _____

    (If not would you like help to make one?) _____

5. Can you read and follow a recipe? _____ Instructions on packets? _____

6. Can you add up a shopping price list? _____

7. Have you made a budget for a week's shopping? _____

8. Which of the following bills have you seen? _____

    Food, clothes, electric, gas, water rates, T.V. licence, council tax, telephone, and rent (as part of a written agreement). Do you understand all/any of them? If not, would you like some help?

    _____

    _____

G. Practical Skills (Shopping)

1. How do you buy your clothes? Circle –

    a) Adult buys them   b) They pay, you choose   c) You shop independently.

2. Do you go food shopping? _____

    Do you choose some of the menus? _____

3. How often do you go and where? _____

4. Have you been food shopping on your own? Where? How often? _____
   _____

H. Managing Money

1. What is your weekly income? (pocket money, earnings?) _____

2. Do you save any? How? _____

3. Do you pay something towards your keep? _____

4. What do you spend the rest on? _____
   _____

5. Are you given any other cash by the adults (e.g: travel, leisure)? _____

6. Do you borrow? How you do pay back? _____

7. Do you spend money on anything you wish that you didn't? What? Would you like help to stop?
   _____

I. Practical Skills (preparing food and cooking)

1. Are you able to use a cooker safely? Gas? Electric? _____

2. Do you help prepare or cook meals? How often? _____

3. Can you cook a hot meal for yourself? What? When? _____

4. Do you plan what you are going to eat so you get a balanced diet? Would you like some help?
   _____

5. Have you been shown how to use a fridge or freezer? (how long food keeps etc)
   _____

6. Do you lay the table? When? _____ Wash up? When? _____
   _____

J. Practical Skills (cleaning)

1. Do you clean/vacuum your room? How often? _____
2. Can you clean a cooker? _____ Fridge? _____
3. Do you clean communal areas? How often? _____ Toilet? _____
4. Who washes your clothes? – Adults/You Alone/Both? _____
5. Who does your ironing? – Adults/You Alone/Both? _____
6. Have you used a launderette? _____
7. Taken shoes to repairers? Clothes to dry cleaners? _____

K. Practical Skills (travelling)

1. Do you travel on public transport? What? When? and How often? _____
   _____
2. Which of these do you do alone? _____
3. Do you walk to the local shops or to town? How often? _____
4. Can you read a bus or train timetable? _____
   (If not would you like help to?) _____
5. How do you travel to school or work? _____
6. Do you get any lifts? Where to? _____
7. Have you passed a cycling proficiency test? _____
8. Do you know if there are any special travel allowances in your area? How do you get them? _____
9. Do you have plans to learn to drive? _____

L. Timekeeping

1. Do you have a watch? _____ If not would you like one? _____
2. Do you have an alarm clock? _____ If not would you like one? _____
3. Do you get up without help? _____
4. Do you keep appointments without being reminded? _____

M. Practical Skills (household)

1. Can you wire a plug? _____ Change a lightbulb or fuse? _____
2. Can you unblock a sink? _____ Know what a stop-cock is? _____
3. Have you sewn on a button? _____ Can you do other simple mending of clothes? _____
4. Read a meter? _____ Check the cost of electricity/water/gas bill? _____
5. Do you use the telephone? _____ Payphone? _____
6. Can you use a calculator? _____ Have you got one? _____
7. Can you weigh and measure? length; weight; fluid? _____
8. Can you do simple first aid? What? _____

N. Health (and health education)

1. Who is your doctor? dentist? _____
2. How do you arrange to see them? _____
3. If you move to another area, you will need to register with another doctor. Do you know how to do this?
   _____
4. Do you know where to find your National Health Card? _____
5. Have you been given enough information on the following? (Circle)

   a) sex education/ contraception   b) HIV/Aids   c) drugs – legal & illegal   d) the police
   e) rights   f) racism   g) religion   h) housing   i) social security

6. By whom, and when? _____
   _____

   Would you like any more information on any of these subjects? _____
7. Do you have books or leaflets on any of the above? Which? Where? _____
   _____
8. Do you have any local telephone numbers where you can make contact about any problems you may have?
   _____
9. Have you someone you can talk to about these topics? _____

O. Privacy

1. Have you keys for – a) the front door?   b) your room?   c) other? _____
2. Do you have your own bedroom? _____
3. Do you have a safe and secure place to keep valuables? Where? _____
4. Do you have somewhere that you consider to be private? _____
5. Are you able to be in and be alone? _____

P. General Information and Rights

1. Are you a member of the library? Do you use it? _____

2. Do you know where these other agencies are? What are their telephone numbers? _____

   a) Police Station   b) Dept. of Social Security
   c) Council Housing Offices   d) Career Office
   e) Employment Service (job centre)   f) Doctors' Surgery
   g) Health Clinic   h) Samaritans
   i) CAB

3. Do you know how to complain if things are not right? _____
   _____

4. Who is your Social Worker? _____

5. Have you their address and telephone number? _____

6. Do you know what to do if stopped by the police or arrested? _____
   _____

7. Do you know you can get free legal advice? Would you like help? _____
   _____

8. Do you know how to get in touch with an appropriate adult? Would you like help? _____
   _____

9. Do you know where to find your Birth Certificate? and National Insurance Number? _____

10. Do you know at what age the law allows you to – a) Smoke   b)   Drink alcohol
    c)   Get married   d)   Have sex   e)   Vote   f)   Appear in Adult Court?

    Stepping Out (See Sheet G2) gives a list of the ages you can do all sorts of things – why not send for a copy?

11. Have you been given Careers Advice – how to apply for a job – use the job centre?
    _____

12. When you are 16 ½ you can put your name on the electoral register. You will then be able to vote when you are 18. Do you know how to get on the register? Do you need help?

Q. Feeling Isolated

1. Do you know where to go for help if you really feel bad about something or someone or just feel lonely?
   _____

2. Have you got an address book with names and telephone numbers in? _____

3. Have you some ideas on how to overcome loneliness? What are they? _____

_____

_____

4. If there is a crisis in your life, such as breaking up with your long standing boy/girl friend, what would you do?

_____

_____

5. Do you know how to go about making new friends? _____

R. Nationality and Ethnicity

1. Do you know what your nationality is? _____

2. If you are not British, do you know if anything needs to be done to sort out your immigration, citizenship and nationality status?

_____

3. Do you have all the documents needed for future dealings over passport, immigration etc.?

_____

4. Do you know who can help?

_____

5. Have you got an up-to-date passport? _____

6. Do you know who will be able to sign the form to support your application for a passport?

_____

7. Do you know which ethnic group you come from?

_____

8. If you come from a minority ethnic group do you need help to meet more people from the same ethnic background?

_____

IS THERE ANYTHING ELSE THAT HAS NOT BEEN ASKED THAT YOU THINK IS IMPORTANT?

_____

_____

_____

_____

(Adapted from Cathcart, J, 1992)

COURT ORDERS AND THE CHILDREN ACT

It may be necessary for the young person to go to court if, for example, their parent(s) and social services can't agree on the best plan for their safety and well-being in the future.

Court orders are only made if something can be achieved by that order, which will be for the good of the young person, and is better than making no order.

You may need to explain to the young person the reasons for going to court, the decisions the court could make and to help them prepare for going to court.

If there is a court order then it will automatically end when a young person is 18 unless it is stopped by the court earlier.

There will also be a guardian ad litem (page 153) appointed by the court to talk about the young person's wishes and feelings plus a solicitor to represent them. They should ensure that the young person's view is heard. An interpreter may also be necessary.

If a young person is being accommodated (see page 142) by the local authority there is no court order.

The court must:

- consider what is best for the young person
- make sure that whatever is to happen, happens as soon as possible
- see that nothing changes unless it's best for the young person

They must consider:

- what the young person wants
- any needs they may have
- what the effect will be on them of any changes
- their age, sex, background or anything else that might be appropriate
- any problems there may have been in the past or are likely to be in future
- the ability of the parent(s)/guardians/carers to meet those needs

On the next pages there is a brief explanation about the various orders that might be imposed.

Ref No: Court orders are outlined in G&R V1

BEING ACCOMMODATED

What does it mean?

This is a technical term where there is no care order. It means that social services provides somewhere for a young person to live if:

- there is no one who has parental responsibility (page 162) for them

    or

- they have been lost or abandoned or have been thrown out of their home

    or

- the person caring for them cannot provide accommodation or care at present

    or

- they might come to harm if they go on living where they are

    or

- they might suffer ill-treatment from another person

    or

- the police or the court have asked social services to provide accommodation for them

Listen to what the young person has to say and whenever possible take notice of their wishes. Try to get them to go back to live at home if it is possible and part of the agreed plan.

At the start of "being accommodated" the young person will often feel scared and wonder what is going on. Tell them simply – you may have to tell them again as they might forget in the crisis.

Talk to them if you can, and try to put them at ease. When they are ready, explain what being accommodated means.

COURT ORDERS – AN OUTLINE SUMMARY OF WHAT THEY MEAN

A CARE ORDER

Is:

- made by the court stating that social services must look after the young person and provide somewhere for them to live. A care order gives social services parental responsibility

- young people must be encouraged to see their family and friends unless the court states otherwise

It is made:

If the court thinks the young person might be:

- suffering significant harm or likely to suffer significant harm and

- the care they are being given is not what a parent should give or they are beyond their parent(s)' control

- if making the order will help the young person

It lasts:

Until one of these happens:

- they are 18; they are adopted; a supervision or residence order is made; the court stops the order; the young person, their parent(s), social services or the person with parental responsibility asks the court to stop the order and the court agrees

INTERIM CARE ORDER

Sometimes an interim care order is made for not more than 8 weeks to give the court time to collect more information. Further ICO's can be made which will last up to four weeks each

The young person may be asked to have a medical examination either physical or psychiatric but they may refuse provided they fully understand.

A CHILD ASSESSMENT ORDER

Is:

- made by the court stating that the parent or those with parental responsibility must take the young person to the specified place e.g. doctor's, hospital, health centre, so the young person may be assessed

It is made:

- where the parent(s) or those responsible have refused to co-operate

- the local authority or authorised person thinks the young person might be in danger of significant harm but the young person is in no immediate danger

if after looking at all the evidence immediate action is needed then an Emergency Protection Order will be made

The young person may be asked to have a medical examination, either physical or psychiatric but they may refuse provided they fully understand what is going on.

CONTACT ORDER

Is:

- made by the court stating who can keep in touch with the young person. It might be their birth parent(s), brothers and sisters, grandparent(s) or anyone who is important to them

you should allow them to visit, stay with them, write to them or speak on the 'phone according to the rules set up by the court

It is made:

- if any of the following ask for it and the court agrees: young person, their parent or guardian, their foster carers if they have been living with them for 3 years or someone close to them. In fact anyone may apply

It lasts:

- until they are 16 or until the court agrees it is no longer necessary. In exceptional circumstances it may last until 18 if the court thinks it is necessary

EMERGENCY PROTECTION ORDER

It is made:

If the court has reason to believe that:

- the young person will come to significant harm if they continue to live where they are or if they are removed from where they are staying

- they are suffering significant harm and their carers will not allow doctors or social workers to see them

The order cannot be stopped or challenged within the first 72 hours. After that it may be challenged in court. It can last up to 8 days and then extended for a further 7 days.

The young person may be asked to have a medical examination, either physical or psychiatric, but they may refuse provided they fully understand what is going on.

FAMILY ASSISTANCE ORDER

Is:

- sometimes made after the young person's parent(s) get divorced

A court welfare officer or someone from social services is appointed to advise, help and befriend the young person, their family, the person caring for them, or the person named on a contact order.

They must be allowed to visit the young person regularly and be told of any change of address.

It lasts:

- for no more than 6 months unless a new order is made

PROHIBITED STEPS ORDER

Is:

- an order made by court stating certain things cannot happen without the court's permission

The court won't make a prohibited steps order if there is a better way of sorting things out or if the young person is already under a care order.

It lasts:

- until the young person is 16 unless there are exceptional reasons for extending it

Ref. No: G&R V1

RESIDENCE ORDER

Is:

- a court order stating where the young person must live

It means:

- the young person must live with whoever is specified in the order and that person will be given parental responsibility if they haven't got it already

- they cannot leave the country for more than a month (nor can they change their surname) without the written permission from whoever has parental responsibility or the court

- any interested party can apply to have it stopped at any time

It lasts:

- usually until the young person is 16 but occasionally until they are 18

SPECIFIC ISSUE ORDER

Is:

- an order made by the court when there is a disagreement about how the young person should be brought up

- it might be about schooling, or religion, or health care etc

It means:

- the court will decide after consulting others what should be done and how it should be done in the interests of the young person

a specific issue order won't be made if there is a better way to sort things out or if there is a care order

It lasts:

- usually no longer than until the young person is 16 years old

the young person's parent(s) or guardian, anyone who has a residence order for them or the person who applied for the first order to be made may apply to have it stopped

SUPERVISION ORDER

Is:

where a supervisor, usually from social services, is appointed to:

- advise, help and befriend a young person and to make sure any other conditions the court set are carried out

It is made:

- when social services are worried that the young person may be suffering harm or is likely to suffer harm because the care they are getting is not what it should be or that they are beyond their parent(s)' control

It lasts:

- usually for 1 year but no longer than three years and not after the young person is 18 years

it can be stopped if a care order is made or if any of the interested parties apply to the court and the court agrees

---

INTERIM SUPERVISION ORDER

Sometimes an interim order is made for up to 8 weeks so that more information can be collected. Another may be issued for a further 4 weeks if necessary.

INDEPENDENT VISITOR

An independent visitor may be appointed if it is:

- thought necessary when the first plan is drawn up
- decided at a review
- the young person agrees

Why do I need an independent visitor?

A young person may benefit from someone else coming to visit them if:

- a young person is not in contact with their parent(s)
- a young person hardly ever sees their parent(s)

    However, if they are in a settled home or foster home and have lots of other friends and visitors it may not be thought necessary

- if it is not possible for a young person to live in a placement with carers of similar background, race or culture then an independent visitor could become a link with a young person's own community

What will independent visitors do?

- they will try to help a young person by advising or befriending them
- they will try to help a young person in their social, emotional, religious or cultural development
- they may advise a young person on any matter they think fit or if the young person asks for help
- in some situations they may act as an advocate, say where the young person feels they are not being cared for properly or their views are not being listened to or considered. They will try to sort out the situation

What type of person are independent visitors?

- someone who can relate to young people
- someone who has their well-being at heart
- they may be only a little older than the young person or much older, say their grandparent's age
- they will be a good listener
- they will be specially chosen to work with young people

How do I get an independent visitor?

- normally the young person's social worker will have details of the procedure or your manager should be able to help

What happens if I don't like the person chosen?

There will be several 'getting to know you' meetings where both the young person and the visitor can decide whether to go ahead with the arrangement.

At all times the young person's best interest and wishes come first.

How long will they keep visiting?

It may be only for a short while until relationships with parent(s) improve or it may go on for several years, it all depends on the circumstances.

It will be discussed at every review.

Will they always visit me?

No, sometimes they will, or the young person may go out and meet them 'on neutral ground', or go on a visit. Occasionally the independent visitor may also invite the young person to their own home. This may of course, be subject to certain controls.

Are independent representatives the same?

An independent representative is **not** the same. An IR is a person who visits young people who are in secure accommodation to ensure the young people are treated fairly and receive suitable care. They are independent both of the secure unit and of the care authority. They will:

- visit every young person as soon as possible after admission and regularly afterwards

- listen to the young person, tell them of their rights, take up matters on behalf of the young person, help them write letters or see the appropriate person

ADOPTION

There are over half a million adopted people living in Britain today. Young people aged 12-18 are not adopted very often. Adoption is usually for the younger child but sometimes young people in the 12-18 age group may want to know about adoption.

An adoption order is a court order.

There will shortly be changes in the Adoption Law. There are also changes taking place in practise in anticipation of the changes.

What happens?

The family they live with may want to adopt the young person or the young person may ask their family to adopt them. In all cases the social worker will talk it through with everyone concerned and fill in the necessary forms.

The family then apply to the court and a guardian ad litem (page 153) or a reporting officer will be appointed to look at all the circumstances and information and then make recommendations to the court.

What does being 'freed for adoption' mean?

It means that the young person has been released from their birth parent(s)' responsibility in preparation for being adopted but must be looked after by social services until the adoption is finalised. It also means that they are 'protected' and no one can do anything until the court decides whether or not an adoption can go through.

What is an adoption panel?

It is a group of between 5 – 10 people including someone from social services, teachers, health visitors, someone from the adoption agency or adoptive parent(s) who meet to make sure:

- the adoption is in the young person's best interest

- the family is suitable to adopt

- the young person is suitable for that family

How long will it take and what will be different?

There is no set time and it will be different every time but if a young person is 'freed' it will be quicker. They must have lived with the family for at least 3 months before adoption procedures begin.

- most adopted young people take the name of their new family

- they will get the same rights and status as any other children in that family

- they will gain extra family such as grandparent(s)

- they won't have a social worker (they can still see him/her but it is most unusual)

- they won't have reviews

- they won't normally see their birth parent(s) but they may have some contact with them if they want to

- they will get a new birth certificate with an adoption entry on it. When they are 18 they can apply to see their original birth certificate

- the new parent(s) will be sent a letter explaining the adoption

An adoption order is a court order and the court decides whether an adoption goes ahead.

What if I want more information?

- Their local social services office may be able to help

- BAAF (British Agencies for Adoption and Fostering), 11 Southwark Street, London, SE1 1RQ – Tel: 071 407 8800

- Post Adoption Centre, 5 Torriano Mews, Torriano Avenue, London, NW5 2RZ – Tel: 071 284 0555

- National Children's Homes, 85 Highbury Park, London, N5 IUD – Tel: 071 226 2033

- National Organisation for Counselling Adoptees and their Parent(s) (Norcap), 3 New High Street, Headington, Oxford OX3 7AJ – Tel: 0865 750554

> In certain circumstances local authorities can provide help to families who want to adopt but are unable to because they are on a low income.

GUARDIAN AD LITEM

Every organisation has its own jargon and social services is no exception.

Words you take for granted within the system may be completely strange for young people. Guardian ad litem is one in question.

What is a guardian ad litem?

'Ad litem' is latin and means 'dealing with the law', so guardian ad litem is a person who has been appointed by the court to look after the interests of a young person if someone has applied for a court order.

What do they do?

They investigate everything about the case. This may involve:

- talking to the young person
- talking to parent(s) or other people who know the young person
- looking at records
- asking advice from other qualified people

In the case of adoption, if the parent(s)/guardian understand and agree to an adoption, a REPORTING OFFICER will be appointed instead. Their job is to make sure that the agreement to adoption is given willingly and that everyone understands fully what is going on. The agreement must be in writing.

In all cases a report written by GAL or RO is given to the court so that the best possible decisions can be made.

Who becomes a guardian ad litem or reporting officer?

Every local authority must have a panel of people who can give independent advice and reports to the court.

Social services can ask people to go on the panel or people can apply themselves. Either way they are interviewed and have to show that they are suitable for the job.

They are usually qualified social workers who do not work for the local authority in question.

GAL must represent the young person's view.

GUARDIANSHIP

Some young people may have a guardian and do not understand what it means. The following might help you explain things.

What is a guardian?

A guardian is a person who is given full parental responsibility for a young person because their parent(s) have died.

The guardian will have the same responsibilities that their parent(s) would have had.

Who can appoint a guardian?

- anyone with parental responsibility (page 162)
- any other guardian
- a court

When does guardianship stop?

- when the young person is 18
- when the court orders it to stop
- when either the young person or someone with parental responsibility applies to the court to have it stopped and the court agrees it is in the interest of the young person

WARDSHIP AND THE INHERENT JURISDICTION

Wardship gives the court continuing responsibility for the young person. The Children Act has reduced the use of wardship.

The use of wardship has diminished because:

- Prohibited Steps Orders
- Specific Issues Orders
- Residence Orders

have largely taken the place of wardship.

Wardship cannot be used when there is a Care Order.

Occasionally the court will use the Inherent Jurisdiction in order to protect a young person. What this means is that the court has retained certain powers to enable it to take action if the need arises and it is in the best interest of the young person.

Local authorities can only use the Inherent Jurisdiction in exceptional circumstances – when the Children Act does not enable the young person to be protected from significant harm.

YOUTH JUSTICE

The present Government is considering changes to the system and penalties of youth justice.

What happens if I break the law?

If a young person breaks the law and the police are involved, the police will take certain action depending on the offence. They try if possible to prevent the young person appearing in court.

1. If it is considered a minor offence, such as riding a bicycle after dark without lights, the police will visit the young person at home in the presence of their parent(s), carer or someone from the duty social services team. The police will warn them.

2. If it is an arrestable offence such as shoplifting, the young person will be taken to the police station for cautioning. The police will contact the young person's parent(s), a relative, carer or someone from the duty social services team.

Youth justice staff (sometimes known as Juvenile Justice staff) may go to the police station when the young person is being interviewed by the police, if their parent(s) or social worker cannot be there or if the young person wants them to be there. The parent(s) can also ask for youth justice staff to be present.

The police keep a young person at the police station for as short a time as possible.

A 'gatekeeping' exercise may also take place. This means that a representative from youth justice, possibly the probation service, social services, the police will meet to discuss what has happened and what should happen in the future. At the moment young people and their parent(s) do not attend these meetings, but this may change in future.

3. If the offence is serious then the young person may go to court. The youth court deals with 11–17 year olds who have committed an offence.

   A gatekeeping exercise will take place before the young person appears in court.

Youth justice staff write pre-sentence reports (previously known as social enquiry reports), will attend youth courts when they act on behalf of social services and the probation service. They will also help the magistrate to decide what is the best course of action.

Note: A 'gatekeeping' exercise takes place (i) if the crime that has been committed is extremely serious (ii) if the young person has had more than one caution. Cautions may be informal at first but if a young person re-offends the caution will be formal – gatekeeping takes place whether the offence is the same each time or if the young person commits different offences. A report will normally be sent to the court.

When sentencing the court must take into account:

- the young person's age
- stage of development of the young person
- seriousness of the offence

What sentence will I get?

The sentence might be:

- discharge
- 'binding over' – which means the young person agrees to keep the peace and/or be of good behaviour
- fine
- compensation order – means the young person must pay for the loss, damage or personal injury he/she has caused
- community service, if 16 or over
- supervision order
- attendance centre order
- probation order, if 16 years or over
- combination order, if 16 or over. This requires the offender to be supervised by a probation officer and to perform community service – the court decides the length of time for each
- curfew
- custody in a young offender institution, if 15 or over

From the age of 16 years, young people may be sentenced as adults.

If a young person commits an offence they may then have a criminal record. This normally lasts for between 6 months and 3 years, depending upon the crime. For exceptionally serious offences such as murder the offender has a criminal record for ever.

What else do youth justice staff do?

They work with all young people who have committed an offence. The staff aim to prevent a young person appearing in court if it is at all possible.

They help young people who are remanded to social services accommodation or custody, while they are waiting for their case to be dealt with. They talk to the young person, explain what is going on, discuss what might happen and also make plans for the young person's future.

They also offer help and support to young people who have been sentenced by the court under, say, a supervision order. This may mean regular reporting to a staff member The young person may also be required to attend at a special session during evenings or weekends.

RECORDS

Many young people see the records social services keep on them as a cause for concern. They do not like people writing things about them that they are not allowed to see.

They also do not like the fact that the records are sometimes left lying around for everyone else to see. They feel they should be kept locked away with only certain people being allowed to read them.

The following questions look at how records should be kept in the light of the Children Act.

What records do social services keep on me?

They may keep 4 sets of records on every young person:

1. A straight-forward list of who is accommodated.

2. Case records.

3. Management records.

4. Looking After Children: Assessment and Action Records which in the future may be mandatory. Some authorities are using them already; others are still testing them and others are not using them at all.

What's on these records?

1. The list shows:

    - the real name of the young person as well as the name they wish to be known by
    - where they are staying
    - their telephone number
    - their date of birth
    - the name of their social worker

    In most authorities this will be kept on the computer and up-dated either by the social worker or by the administrative assistant.

2. Case records – as well as the above information these should show:

    - details of their family
    - their plan
    - any reports written about them such as court reports, health, home study etc
    - review documents
    - details of court orders
    - details of arrangements made for contact with their family
    - any special arrangements
    - any documents used to find out more about the young person such as psychological report or court report

    The young person may also ask to have other documents such as certificates or school reports to be kept with this information.

    Children's homes keep records about the young person and these are usually very similar to the case records.

    Foster carers are sometimes given only brief written documents about a young person. This depends on the practice of the local authority. However, it is a good idea for them to keep their own records for future reference. This could be in the form of a foster carer's diary, listing events, illnesses, accidents as well as specific details about the young person.

    If the foster carer is involved with the young person's court case or accompanies the young person to court they may be given a copy of the court order.

3. Management records – these will be the same as case records except that details of their carer(s) will be included.

4. Looking After Children: Assessment and Action Records – these are a set of questions covering:

- health
- education
- identity
- family and social relationships
- social presentations
- emotional and behavioural development
- self-care skills

which young people should help complete. These records are used to make sure every step possible is being taken to try to ensure the young person is developing to the best of their ability. Carers must discuss with the young person many topics – 'Answers' may be helpful here.

At the back of these records there is a summary of what action needs to be taken and by whom.

Can I see them?

Every young person has a right to see their records if they wish. There must be a very good reason for anyone saying no. Some records are written by other agencies and cannot be made available to them.

When a young person sees their records for the first time, what is written may come as quite a shock and they may need help to cope with this.

What do I have to do to see them?

In the past young people have not been allowed to see them so it has come as quite a shock for some social workers and carers to have to change.

Some local authorities have introduced systems to make sure only certain people see the records. This, unfortunately, has also made it difficult for the young people to see them.

If the young person wants to see them you will have to find out what the system is and help them follow it.

Who else can see them?

All these records are confidential with only authorised staff able to see them.

The Case Records and the Management records should be held in a safe place so that only those people shown below may see them:

- the young person's social worker, superiors and the young person
- a government inspector
- the young person's guardian ad litem

How long will the records be kept?

The computer records are kept until the young person is 23, or if they die before that, for 5 years after their death.

Case records must be kept for 75 years from the date they were started; or for 15 years after the young person's death if they die before they are 18 years old.

PARENTAL RESPONSIBILITY

What is it?

By law there are certain things parent(s) should and should not do when bringing up a young person. They must ensure that a young person gets correct medical treatment, full education, and that their physical, moral and religious needs are met.

Who has parental responsibility?

If a young person's father and mother were married to each other when they were born, or have since married, they both automatically have parental responsibility.

What if my parent(s) didn't get married?

- only the mother has parental responsibility automatically
- if the father was not married to the mother he can:
    - apply to the court for parental responsibility or
    - draw up a formal agreement with their mother which must be registered with the High Court in London or
    - ask to be made their guardian or
    - be granted a residence order by the court

Who else can get parental responsibility?

- parent(s) can delegate it to someone else, but they won't lose it themselves
- an adoptive parent automatically gets parental responsibility
- a guardian
- the person with whom the young person is living if a residence order is made
- the local authority gets it if a care order or emergency protection order is made

How long does parental responsibility last?

Until a young person is 18, but a court order may cancel it before then.

CHANGING NAMES

Many young people want to be called by a different name for many reasons such as:

bad memories of their father or mother, or of their step father or mother; to try to create a new identity; because its easier to be known by the name of the rest of the family – this often happens when young people are fostered – or just because they simply don't like the name they've got.

I want to change my name. Can I?

Yes. Whatever the reason a young person can do this simply by asking other people to call them by any name they wish.

If a young person wants to change their name for legal purposes then they can do so by **deed poll** or **statutory declaration**. In either case this means going to a solicitor. This proves to others that they have changed their name. There will be a charge for this work, and young people should find out what it is before instructing the solicitor to proceed.

What happens if I am on a care order or residence order?

Young people can change their first name at any time, but to change their surname they must have the written permission of whoever has parental responsibility for them or the court.

Why should I bother to go to court to change my name?

As we said earlier there is nothing to stop anyone changing their name but if a young person decides that the change is permanent then it is better to do it formally. If they don't it may cause problems later in life, for example, if they want to join the armed forces.

The Citizens Advice Bureaux should be able to give more details.

ANSWERS – SUGGESTION SHEET

This book has been written in partnership with young people and their carers.

We would like to continue this partnership by asking you to let us know of any other topics you think might be included in a future edition.

We hope to produce a further book for residential and foster carers of children under 11 years of age. We would also like your suggestions on what might be included.

Please tear out this page, write your suggestions on it and return it to The Department of Social Work Studies, University of Southampton, Highfield, Southampton, SO9 5NH.

My suggestions for a future ANSWERS book are:

My suggestions for a book for carers of Children under 11 years of age are:
(please delete as appropriate)

USEFUL TELEPHONE NUMBERS AND ADDRESSES

General

CCETSW (Central Council for Education and Training in Social Work)
Derbyshire House
St. Chad's Street
London WC1H 8AD
Tel: 071 278 2455

CCETSW is a UK wide statutory organisation responsible for promoting and approving education and training for social work and social care staff in the personal social services

BAAF
(British Agencies for Adoption and Fostering)
11 Southwark Street
London, SE1 1RQ
Tel: 071 407 8800

BAAF promotes public understanding of adoption and fostering; develops high standards of practice amongst child care and other professionals; provides high quality training tailored to meet specific needs; acts as an independent voice in the field of child care to inform and influence policy-makers.

National Children's Home/Careline
12 Romney Place
Maidstone
Kent ME15 6LE
Tel: 0622 756677

Careline listens to young peoples' concerns, complaints, and representations made on their behalf, about the care they are receiving from social services. Careline try to resolve the problem or will investigate formal complaints on behalf of the young person.

A Voice for the Child in Care
Unit 4, Pride Court,
80-82 White Lion Street
London N1 9PF
Tel: 071 833 5792

A Voice for the Child in Care provides an independent person service for the Child Act complaints procedure; gives advice about the use of the complaints procedure; provides an independent representative service for young people in secure accommodation and can provide an independent person for secure accommodation review panels.

Family Rights Group
The Print House
18 Ashwin Street
London E8 3DL
Tel: 071 923 2628

The Family Rights Group offers an advice line for parents, relatives and carers who have children and young people in contact with social service departments on a Child Protection Register.

Who Cares? Trust
235 Goswell Road
London EC1V 7JD
Tel: 071 833 9047

Who Cares? offer a practical service for young people on health; education; counselling; employment and information. They communicate with 20,000 young people through the Who Cares? magazine published quarterly.

National Children's Bureau
8 Wakley Street
London EC1V 7QE
Tel: 071 278 9441

This organisation carries out research and influences policy and practice on matters relating to young people and families. They may be able to answer your general questions or pass you on to someone who can.

NFCA (National Foster Care Association)
Leonard House
5–7 Marshalsea Road
London SE1 1EP
Tel: 071 828 6266

NFCA aims to improve the quality of care for children and young people who are in foster care in the UK. It seeks to ensure that competent foster carers, adequately supported, trained and managed by fostering agencies, are available for all the children and young people who might benefit from this form of care.

Many of these organisations offer good value information material.

Specific

Abuse

Childline
Freepost 1111
London N1 0BR
Tel: 0800 1111 (freephone)

Kidscape
82 Brook Street
London W1Y 1YG
Tel: 071 730 3300

Adoption

Post Adoption Centre
5 Torriano Mews
Torriano Avenue
London NW5 2RZ
Tel: 071 284 0555

National Children's Homes
85 Highbury Park
London N5 1UD
Tel: 071 226 2033

National Organisation for Counselling
Adoptees and their Parent(s) (Norcap)
3 New Street
Headington
Oxford OX3 7AJ
Tel: 0865 750554

BAAF
(British Agencies for Adoption and Fostering)
11 Southwark Street
London SE1 1RQ
Tel: 071 407 8800

Aids/HIV

Aids Information Service will
send leaflets
0800 555777

National Advisory Aids Helpline will
talk or give counselling
0800 567123
Barnado's work with HIV/AIDS
Tanner's Lane
Barkingside
Ilford
Essex IG6 1QG
Tel: 081 550 8822

Alcohol

Alcoholics Anonymous
P.O. Box 1
Stonebrow House
Stonebrow
York YO1 2NJ
Tel: 0904 644026

Alcohol Concern
275 Grays Inn Road
London WC1X 8QF
Tel: 071 833 3471
For the family and friends of
problem drinkers

Al Anon Family Groups
61 Dover Street
London SE1 4YR
Tel: 071 403 0888

Bereavement

Cruse Bereavement Care
Cruse House
126 Sheen Road
Richmond
Surrey TW9 1UR
Tel: 081 940 4818

Care

A.S.C. Tel: 0800 616101 (freephone)
(Advocacy Service for Children)

First Key (Aftercare)
Oxford Chambers
Oxford Place
Leeds LS1 3AX
Tel: 0532 443898/432541

Black in Care
Elin House
86 Bellender Road
London SE15 4RG

N.A.Y.P.I.C.
(National Association of Young People in Care)
Unit 94
23 New Mount Street
Manchester M4 4DE
Tel: 061 953 4041/4107

N.A.Y.P.I.C.
8a Stucley Place
Camden
London NW8 8NJ
Tel: 071 284 4793

NSPCC
(National Society for the Prevention of Cruelty to Children)
67 Saffron Hill
London EC1N 8RS
Tel: 071 242 1626

BAAF
(British Agencies for Adoption and Fostering)
11 Southwark Street
London SE1 1RQ
Tel: 071 407 8800

NFCA
(National Foster Care Association)
Leonard House
5-7 Marshalsea Road
London SE1 1EP
Tel: 071 828 6266

Deafness

The Royal National Institute for Deaf People
105 Gower Street
London WC1E 6AH
Tel: 071 387 8033

British Deaf Association
38 Victoria Place
Carlisle
Cumbria CA1 1HU
Tel: 0228 48844

Debt

National Debtline
318 Summer Lane
Birmingham B19 3RL
Tel: 021 359 8501

Depression

The Samaritans
10 The Grove
Slough SL1 1QP
Tel: 0753 532713

SANE (Schizophrenia and National Emergency)
199-205 Old Marylebone Road
London NW1 5QP
Tel: 071 724 8000 – Helpline

Discrimination/Racism

Black Issues Project (BAAF)
11 Southwick Street
London SE1 1RQ
Tel: 071 407 8800

The Commission for Racial Equality
Elliot House
10-12 Allington Street
London SW1E 5EH
Tel: 071 828 7022

The Commission has regional offices in Birmingham, Manchester, Leicester and Leeds.

Institute of Race Relations
2-6 Leeke Street
London WC1X 9HS
Tel: 071 837 0041

The Equal Opportunities Commission
Overseas House
Quay Street
Manchester M3 3HN
Tel: 061 833 9244

Runnymede Trust
11 Princelet Street
London E1 6QH
Tel: 071 375 1496

Disability

R.A.D.A.R. (Royal Association for Disability and Rehabilitation)
25 Mortimer Street
London W1N 8AB
Tel: 071 637 5400

British Deaf Association
38 Victoria Place
Carlisle
Cumbria CA1 1HU
Tel: 0228 48844

British Epilepsy Association
Anstey House
40 Hanover Square
Leeds LS3 18E
Tel: 0532 439393

British Sports Association for the Disabled
Solecast House
13-27 Brunswick Place
London N1 6DX
Tel: 071 490 4919

Disabled Living Foundation
380-384 Harrow Road
London W9 2HU
Tel: 071 289 6111

Guide Dogs for the Blind
Hillfields
Burghfield
Reading RG7 3YG
Tel: 0734 835555

Royal National Institute for the Blind
Gt. Portland Street
London W1N 6AA
Tel: 071 3881266

Riding for the Disabled
Avenue R
National Agricultural Centre
Kenilworth
Warwickshire CV8 2LY
Tel: 0203 696510

Spastics Society
12 Park Crescent
London W1
Tel: 071 636 5020

Spinal Injuries Association
Newpoint House
76 St. James Lane
London N10 3DE
Counselling – 081 883 4296 (Direct line)
General enquiries – 081 444 2121

Drug Abuse

SCODA (The Standing Conference on Drug Abuse)
1 Hatton Place
Hatton Garden
London EC1N 8ND
Tel: 071 430 2341

Release (Legal and Drugs Advice)
– runs a national 24-hour emergency telephone service, particularly useful if someone has been arrested for a drug offence.
388 Old Street
London EC1V 9LT
Emergency Tel: 071 603 8654
Mon – Fri 10am – 6pm 071 729 9904

Adfam is a national charity for the families and friends of drug users. There is a Helpline offering confidential advice and counselling week day afternoons 1.00–4.30pm
Tel: 071 498 4680

Eating

Eating Disorders Association
Sackville Place
44-48 Magdalen Street
Norwich NR3 1JE
Tel: 0603 621414

Vegetarian Society
Parkdale
Dunham Road
Altringham
Cheshire WA14 4QG
Tel: 061 928 0793

Health

British Heart Foundation
14 Fitzharding Street
London W1H 4DH
Tel: 071 935 0185

Health Education Authority
Hamilton House
Mabledon Place
London WC1H 9TX
Tel: 071 383 3833

Housing/Homelessness

Shelter
Housing Aid Information Team
88 Old Street
London EC1V 9HU
Tel: 071 253 0202

Law

Children's Legal Centre
20 Compton Terrace
London N1 2UN
Tel: 071 359 6251

Listening

The Samaritans
10 The Grove
Slough SL1 1QP
Tel: 0753 532713
      071 284 4793

Ombudsmen

Greater London, Kent, Surrey,
East and West Sussex
Dr. D. C. M. Yardley
Local Government Ombudsman
21 Queen Anne's Gate
London SW1H 9BU
Tel: 071 222 5622

The South West, the West, the South, East Anglia
and most of Central England
Mr. E. B. C. Osmotherley
Local Government Ombudsman
The Oaks
Westwood Way
Westwood Business Park
Coventry CV4 8JB
Tel: 0203 695999

The East Midlands and the North of England
Mrs. P. A. Thomas
Local Government Ombudsman
Beverley House
17 Shipton Road
York YO3 6FZ
Tel: 0904 630151

Pregnancy/Contraception

British Pregnancy Advisory Service
160 Shepherd's Bush Road
Hammersmith
London W6 7PB
Tel: 071 602 3804

Family Planning Association (UK)
27-35 Mortimer Street
London W1N 7RJ
Tel: 071 636 7866

Solvent Abuse

Re-Solv
30A High Street
Stone
Staffordshire ST15 8AW
Tel: 0785 817885

Institute Study of Drug Dependence (ISDD)
1 Hatton Place off St. Cross Street
London EC1N 8ND
Tel: 071 430 1993

Sex/Sexuality

Brook Advisory Centres
153a East Street
London SE17 2SD
Tel: 071 708 1234

Family Planning Association
27-35 Mortimer Street
London W1N 7RJ
Tel: 071 636 7866

Lesbian and Gay Switchboard
Tel: 071 837 7324

Smoking

Smokebusters
Redland Hill
Bristol BS6 6UZ
Tel: 0272 238317 (England)

Ash (Action on Smoking and Health)
109 Gloucester Place
London W1H 3PH
Tel: 071 935 3519

Ash (Action on Smoking and Health)
372a Cowbridge Road East
Canton
Cardiff CF5 1HF
Tel: 0222 641101

Training

CCETSW
(Central Council for Education and Training in Social Work)
Derbyshire House
St. Chad's Street
London WC1 8AD
Tel: 071 278 2455

BAAF
(British Agencies for Adoption and Fostering)
11 Southwark Street
London SE1 1RQ
Tel: 071 407 8800

Youth Justice

Young Offender Community Support Scheme
Ashwood
Ashwood Road
Woking
Surrey GU22 7JR
Tel: 0483 769229

Local

Citizens Advice Bureau

Doctors

Samaritans

Dentists

Family Planning Clinic

Opticians

Brook Advisory Centre

ACKNOWLEDGEMENTS

First and foremost I would like to thank Clare Roskill, Programme Head, Child Care, CCETSW, for recommending that CCETSW should fund the initial stage of the project including the evaluation. Clare has also been a very thorough critical reader who gave many helpful suggestions for improving the book.

We would also like to thank the Fishmongers' Company for initial starter funding and Christine Hammond, Director of BAAF for supporting the project.

I would especially like to thank the following members of the working party who helped tremendously with their comments, criticisms and suggestions. Their broad experiences and diverse backgrounds were invaluable to their contribution: Morag Currie, residential social services officer, Hampshire; Sue Williams, foster carer, Berkshire; Angela MacDonald, residential carer, Berkshire; Leanne McMulkin, ex childrens home, Hampshire; Nigel Ferguson, ex foster care, Berkshire; Beverley Ferguson, in foster care, Berkshire; Verity Denman, in foster care, Berkshire; Alia Hassan, black disabled trainer, Hampshire; Pamela Mundy, private residential manager: Five Rivers Project, Wiltshire; Mike Earl, children's home manager, Hampshire; Ray Coker, black trainer and practice teacher for residential carers. Previously residential worker at Turner's Court, Berkshire.

I would also like to thank the following critical readers/advisers

Kish Bhatti-Sinclair, Lecturer, Department of Social Work Studies, University of Southampton; Vanessa Cleal Principal Training Officer, Child Care, Hampshire Social Services Department; Ann Doyle CCETSW, Welsh Office; Ruth Forrester, Area Care Manager, Powys Social Services; Steve Harwood, Principal Policy & Practice Officer, Barnardos; Peter Holmes, Senior Health Promotions Officer, Health Promotion Service, Southampton; Gill Jones, Children's Rights Officer, Birmingham; Barbara Kahan, National Children's Bureau; Tory Laughland, Editor, Who Cares? Magazine; Jonathan Montgomery, University of Southampton, Faculty of Law; Peter Morey, First Key; Lily Robertson, Social Work Education Adviser, CCETSW, London and South-East Office, Shaila Shah, BAAF, London; Frances Sheldon, Macmillan Lecturer in Psycho-social Pallative Care, Department of Social Work Studies, University of Southampton; Heather Stephenson, Assistant Co-ordinator, Independent Representative Service, Voice of the Child in Care; Daphne Walder, Home Tutor, Hampshire Education Department; Harriet Ward, Research Fellow, Dartington Social Research Unit, University of Bristol – Looking after Children Project.

The draft of Answers was evaluated by residential and foster carers in

● Powys ● Havering ● Derby ● Birmingham ● Berkshire ● Hampshire

and also students at the University of Southampton, University of Bournemouth and Southampton Institute of Higher Education.

A particular thanks must go to all these people.

I WOULD ALSO LIKE TO THANK HAMPSHIRE COUNTY COUNCIL FOR ALLOWING US TO USE MATERIAL FROM THEIR GUIDEBOOK FOR YOUNG PEOPLE

We would like to acknowledge the following organisations who have given permission for their material to be reproduced as noted within the text – Family Planning Association Magazine, *Just 17*, 1993, D Gambe, J Gomes, V Kapur, M Rangel, P Stubbs *Improving Practice with Children and Families*, 1992, Health Education Authority, *That's the Limit*, 1992, National Foster Care Association, *Stepping Out*, 1993, M A Porteous *Porteous Problem Checklist, An Inventory of Adolescent Problems*, 1985, Who Cares? Magazine, *Issues 23 and 25*, 1993.

SOURCES OF REFERENCE

In researching for, and compiling this handbook a wide range of material was used. I would like to acknowledge the following:

Access to Personal Files (Social Services), Regulations 1989, HMSO
Aldgate J, Maluccio A and Reeves C 1989, *Adolescents in Foster Families*, BAAF/Batsford
Aldgate J and Simmonds J (eds) 1988, *Direct Work with Children*, BAAF/Batsford
BAAF training materials 1991, *Children who Foster*, BAAF
Barn R 1993, *Black Children in the Public Care System*, BAAF/Batsford
Barnardos 1992, *Barnardo's Work with HIV/AIDS*, Barnados
Batty D and Bayley N 1984, *In Touch with Children*, BAAF training pack
Batty D 1993, *HIV Infection and Children in Need*, BAAF
Bower S and G H 1991, *Asserting Yourself, A Practical Guide for Positive Change*, Addison-Wesley
British Agencies for Adoption and Fostering 1990/92/93, *Leaflets on Adoption and Fostering. A Range of Leaflets on Essential Areas in Adoption and Fostering*, BAAF
British Agencies for Adoption and Fostering 1987/89/90, *Range of Workbooks for Use with Children and Young People*, BAAF
British Heart Foundation 1988, *Smoking and your Heart*, BHF
British Pregnancy Advisory Service, *Who can I turn to?* BPAS
Bullock R, Little M and Millham S 1993, *Going Home, The Return of Children Separated from their Familes*, Dartmouth
Buchanan A 1993, M.Sc Diploma in Social Work Studies, *Child Protection Handbook for Students*, University of Southampton
Buchanan A, Wheal A, Walder D, Macdonal S and Coker R 1993, *Answering Back, Report by Young People Being Looked After Under the Children Act 1989*, Department of Social Work Studies, University of Southampton
Buchanan A (ed) (in press) 1989, *Partnership in Practice, the Children Act, 1989*, Avebury
Cathcart James, MSc Thesis 1992, *Leaving Care from Therapeutic Communities*, University of Southampton, Department of Social Work Studies
CCETSW 1993, *Qualifications for Carers*, CCETSW
CCETSW 1992, *Residential Child Care in the Diploma in Social Work. Guidance on Knowledge, Values Skills and Competence*, CCETSW
CCETSW 1992, *Setting Quality Standards for Residential Care, A Practical Way Forward*, CCETSW
CCETSW 1991, *The Teaching of Child Care in the Diploma in Social Work*, CCETSW
Children's Legal Centre 1987, *Education Rights Handbook: Advisers Guide to the Legal Rights of School Students*, Children's Legal Centre
Department for Education 1992, *Exclusions*, HMSO
Department of Health, Parker R, Ward H, Jackson S Aldgate J, Wedge P 1991, *Looking After Children, Assessing Outcomes in Child Care*, HMSO
Department of Health 1993, *Looking After Children, Assessment and Action Records*, HMSO
Department of Health 1991, *Looking After Children, Guidelines for Users of Assessment and Action Records*, HMSO
Department of Health 1989, *The Care of Children; Principles and Practice*, HMSO
Department of Health 1990, *An Introduction to the Children Act*, HMSO
Department of Health 1990, *Protecting Children: A Guide for Social Workers Undertaking a Comprehensive Assessment*, HMSO

Department of Health 1991, *Patterns and Outcomes in Care in Child Placement*, HMSO
Department of Health 1991, *The Children Act 1989 – range of leaflets and guides for parents and young people*, HMSO
Department of Health 1991, *Children Act 1989. Guidance and Regulations, Volume 1*, HMSO
Department of Health 1991, *Children Act 1989, Guidance and Regulations, Volume 2*, HMSO
Department of Health 1991, *Children Act 1989, Guidance and Regulations, Volume 3*, HMSO
Department of Health 1991, *Children Act 1989, Guidance and Regulations, Volume 4*, HMSO
Department of Health 1991, *Children Act 1989, Guidance and Regulations, Volume 6*, HMSO
Department of Health 1991, *Children Act 1989, Guidance and Regulations, Volume 7*, HMSO
Department of Health 1991, *Children Act 1989, Guidance and Regulations, Volume 8*, HMSO
Department of Health 1991, *Children Act 1989, Guidance and Regulations, Volume 9*, HMSO
Department of Health 1991, *Children Act 1989, Guidance and Regulations, Index*, HMSO
Department of Health 1991, *Working Together under the Children Act 1989, A Guide to Arrangements for Interagency Co-operation for the Protection of Children from Abuse*, HMSO
Department of Health October 1992, *Drugs Publication*, Department of Health
Department of Health 1992, *Solvents, A Parent's Guide*, Department of Health
Department of Health 1993, *Guidance on Permissible Forms of Control in Children's Residential Care*, HMSO
Department of Health 1993, *The Law Relating to Child Support*, HMSO
Eating Disorders Association, *Eating Disorders*, EDA
Employee Harassment 1991, *Policy & Procedure for Progressing Complaints*, Southampton City Council
Family Planning Association 1992, *Factsheets, 3E,4B,5A,5C,5E*, FPA
Family Planning Association/Health Education Authority,1991, *Your Guide to Safer Sex and the Condom*, HEA
Family Planning Association 1991, *Sexuality, Information for Young People*, FPA
Family Planning Association 1993, *Your Guide to Contraception*, FPA
Family Rights Group 1991, *The Children Act 1989, Working in Partnership with Families*, HMSO
Gambe D, Gomes J, Kapur V, Rangel M, Stubbs P 1992, *Improving Practice with Children and Families*, CCETSW
Gillick v *West Norfolk and Wisbech Area Health Authority 1986*, AC112
Gunn M J 1991, *Sex and the Law*, Family Planning Association
Hampshire County Council 1991, *My Guidebook*, Ashford Open Learning
Hampshire Social Services Department 1992, *The A - Z of Foster Care*, HCC
Hampshire Social Services Department 1993, *Hampshire Secure Accommodation*, HCC
Health Education Authority 1991, *Smoking the Facts*, HEA
Health Education Authority circa 1990, *What to do about Glue Sniffing*, HEA
Health Education Authority 1992, *Guide to Healthy Sex Life*, HEA
Incomes Data Services Ltd 1992, *Combating Harassment at Work*, Income Data Services
Kahan B 1993, *Residential Care for Children, Report of a Department of Health Seminar held on 30 October and 1 November 1991 at Dartington Hall, Devon*, HMSO
Kent Mount Associates 1992/3 Training Materials, KMA
Leicester City Council 1991, *Healthy Leicester 2000*, Leicester City Council
Layzell S 1993, *Staying Safe and Drug Use*, Scoda
Levy A & Kahan B 1991, *The Pindown Experience and Protection of Children*, Staffordshire County Council
Macaskill C 1991, *Adopting or Fostering a Sexually Abused Child*, BAAF/Batsford

McCartt Hess P, Ohman Proch K 1993, Contact: *Managing Visits to Children Looked After Away from Home*, BAAF

McWhinnie A, Batty D 1993, *Children of Incest Whose Secret is it?*, BAAF

Millham S, Bullock R, Hosie K and Little M 1986, *Lost in Care. The Problem of Maintaining Links between Children in Care and their Families*, Gower

NACRO 1993, *Criminal Justice Act 1991 – Young People and the Youth Court*, NACRO

National Foster Care Association 1991, *Questions and Answers about fostering Leaflet*, (also published in Gujarati, Urdu, Punjabi and Bengali), NFCA

National Foster Care Association 1991, *Fostering Children with Disabilities*, NFCA

National Foster Care Association 1991, *Fostering Teenagers*, NFCA

National Foster Care Association 1993, *Aftercare: Making the Most of Foster Care*, NFCA

National Foster Care Association 1993, *Working with Parents*, leaflet, NFCA

National Foster Care Association, *Signposts, a Range of Leaflets on Complex Areas of Foster Care*, NFCA

National Foster Care Association 1993, *Stepping Out*, NFCA

Newell P 1991, *The UN Convention and Children's Rights in the UK*, National Children's Bureau

NCVQ 1993, *NVQs and Careers Guidance*, NCVQ

NCVQ 1993 *NVQ, a Brief Guide*, NCVQ

NCVQ *Information Note April 1993*, General National Vocational Qualifications, NCVQ

NCVQ 1993, *The NVQ Monitor, Autumn*, NCVQ

NSPCC, *Protect Your Child – A Guide about Child Abuse for Parents*, NSPCC

The Open University Pack, *The Children Act 1989, Putting it into Practice*, OU

Phab Hampshire Project, *Teachers' Notes on Physical Disability*, Phab, Hampshire Project

Porteous, M A 1985, *Porteous Problem Checklist, An Inventory of Adolescent Problems*, NFER-Nelson

Race Relations Act 1976, HMSO

Re-Solv 1991, *What Every Parent Needs to Know About Solvent Abuse*, The Society for the Prevention of Drug Abuse

Ryan T and Walker R 1993, *Life Story Work*, BAAF

Sex Discrimination Act 1975, HMSO

Social Services Inspectorate 1992, *Concern for Quality, The First Annual Report of the Chief Inspector, Social Services Inspectorate 1991/1992*, HMSO

Southampton City Council 1992, *Personnel Policies & Procedures*, Southampton City Council

Southampton Health Promotion Services 1993, *Outlands Oracle*, Southampton Health Promotion Service

Stainton Rogers W, Hevey D and Ash E 1989, *Child Abuse and Neglect Facing the Challenge*, Batsford

The Children Act 1989, HMSO

Triseliotis J and Marsh P 1993, *Prevention and Reunification*, BAAF/Batsford

Utting W 1991, *Children in the Public Care, A Review of Residential Child Care*, HMSO

University of Southampton, Merton & Sutton 1990, *Child Protection*, University of Southampton

Wessex Regional Health Authority 1992, *Eat Well, Be Well*, Wessex Regional Health Authority

Who Cares? 1993 *Magazine, Issues 23 and 25*, Who Cares?

Who Cares? Magazine/Social Work Today 1991, *The Independent Person's Address Book*, Who Cares?

Winchester Health Authority 1993, *Confusion, booklet of advice for young people*, Winchester Health Authority

United Nations 1989, *The Convention on the Rights of the Child*, UNICEF

INDEX

A (Advanced levels), 49
ABC analysis of behaviour, 83
Abuse, effects of, 103
    emotional, 103
    how to help young people, 103
    identifying, 103
    physical, 103
    sexual, 103
    signs of, 103
    what to do if suspected, 104
Abusers, who are they, 103
Accommodated, what it means, 142
Acid, 64
Adoption, 151
    adoption law, changes due, 151
    adoption panel, 151
Aftercare, preparation and planning, 111
    training for, 113
    what help is there, 11
    what is needed, 110
AIDS/HIV, 70
Alcohol, 57
    measuring units, 57
    what to do if a young person is drunk, 58
Anorexia Nervosa, 55
Arty things, what can I do, 51
AS (Advanced Supplementary level), 49
Assessment and Action Records, 158, 159
Baby-sitting, can I stay overnight, 75
Barnados, 33
Behaviour,
    encouraging positive, 83
    importance of young people accepting responsibility, 84
    knowing what is allowed, acceptable, 83
    spotting positive, 83
Being looked after,
    needs of young people on admission, 10
Bereavement and loss, 108
Billy, 64
Black experiences of being in care, 29
BAAF, British Association of Adoption and Fostering, 164, 165
    contact with parents, 21
    life story work, 25
Breaking the law, possible sentences, 157
    youth justice, 156
Brown, 64

BTEC Higher National, 50
Budgeting, 39-40
Bulimia nervosa, 55
Bullied, what can I do, 107
Bullies, 107
Bullying, 91, 107
Cannabis, 64
Care order, 143
    and changing names, 163
Care, when can I leave, 111
Careers
    Advisory Service, 126
    office, 126
    how to find out what is available, 126
Carers responsibilities, 4
    young people's views, 5
Case records, 159
Catholic Children's Homes, 33
CCETSW, 6, 172, 175
Changing names, 163
Cheating, 91
Checklists and forms, permission to photocopy, 2
Child Assessment Order, 144
Child guidance workers, 9
Child protection conference, 19
    how often are meetings held, 20
    what is it, 19
    who gets a copy of the minutes, 19
    what happens, 19
    who goes, 19
Child protection procedures, 106
Child protection register, what is it, 20
    why is there a list, 20
Child Support Agency, 71-72
Children's homes, what are they, 33
Children's rights officer, 9
Child protection, 103-105
Citizens Advice Bureau, help with discrimination, harassment, 31
Clubs, finding one, 51
Commission for Racial Equality, help with discrimination, harassment, 31
Communication, behaviour as a way of, 83
Complaints, under the Children Act, 26
Condoms for men and women, 58
Confidence, building it in young people, 88
Confidentiality, 87

178

Contact Order, 144
Contact with families, 21, 22
    benefits, 23
    importance of plan, 21
    keeping a record, 23
    measures to help, 22
Control, encouraging positive behaviour, 83
    positive methods, 85
Contraception, 58
Court orders and the Children Act 141-147
    what a court must consider, 141-147
Crisis, coping with, 96
Cruelty 91
Culture, 29-30
CV (Curriculum Vitae), preparing one for a job application, 122
Debt counselling, 40
Deceit, 91
Decision making, 79-82
    for and against checklist, 81
Degree courses, 50
Diet, importance in health, 55
Differences, meeting needs, 30
    recognising, respecting, 29, 30
Diploma in Social Work, 7
Directors of social services, 9
Disabled people and sex, 74
Disabled Persons (Employment) Act 1944, 1958, 28
Discipline, young people's views, 84
Discrimination, what does it mean, 28
    direct, 28
    indirect, 28
    how carers can help, 31
    rejecting it, 91
    types of, 28
    victimisation, 28
Dove, 64
Drug abuse, 63
    how to minimize harm, 69
    how to prevent, 65
    reasons for, 63
    risk of Hepatitis B, 65
    risk of HIV, 65
    what to do if high, 65
    what to do in an emergency, 65
    what to look for, 63
    where to get help, 65

Drugs, types, 64
"E", 64
Eating disorders, 55
Ecstasy, 64
Education welfare officer, 9
Education, 43
    a young person's checklist, 45
    ideas to help young people, 44
Educational psychologist, 9
Emergency Protection Order, 145
Emotional problems, 102-109
Equal Opportunities Commission, 31
Exercise, importance, 54
Expenses, cutting down on, 40
    cutting out smoking, 40
Facts of life, 71
Family Assistance Order, 145
Family based carer, 8
Family history, does a young person know, 134
Family placement worker, 9
Family planning, 58
Field social worker, 8, 15, 18, 19, 21, 25, 32, 44, 75, 111
First Key, 113
Football team, benefits of, 53
Foster carer, 8
    who are they, 32
Fostered, how does it work, 32
    what does it mean, 32
Friends, making and keeping, 94
    making new ones, 94
    staying with, 75
GAL or RO, 153
Gay men, 74
GCSE, 46-50
GNVQ, 45-50
Go Fast, 64
Grass, 64
Group living, 95
Growing up, 78
Guardian ad Litem, 153
    what they do, 153
Guardianship, 154
Guidance and Regulations, section noted at foot of most pages, 1
Gurudaware, 31
"H", 64

Hallucinogens, 64
Harm, how to minimize in drug and solvent abuse, 69
Health Promotion Units, 59
Health Record Sheet, 61
Health, 54-62
Health, confidentiality, 59
    how to keep, 54
    keeping a record, 60
    why is it important, 54
    medicals, right for a young person to refuse, 59
Helpers for young people, 8
Henry, 64
Hepatitis B, 65
Heroin sub, 64
Heroin, 64
Hindu temple, 31
HIV, risk with drug abuse, 65
HIV/AIDS, 70
HIV: how virus is passed on, 70
Home environment, what can I do in my room, 35
    what young people can do to help, 35
Home, children returning after being looked after, 21
Housing, 114
    checklist, 116
    what to think about, 114
    where to live, 114
Indecent exposure, what is it, 71
Independence on leaving care, 112
Independent representatives, who are they, 150
Independent visitor, 9, 148
    what they do, 148
    when they are offered, 148
Independence, ready for it, 132-140
Interim Care Order, 143
Interim Supervision Order, 147
Interviews, preparing for, 123
    questions that may be asked, 124
Isolated or lonely, 130
Job, applying for one, 118
    choosing one, 117
    finding one, 118
    writing an application letter, 120
    part time, 76
    preparing for interviews, 124
Juvenile Justice, 156
Key worker, 8
Know yourself checklist, 89
Language, linguistic background, 29

Law, what happens if I break the law, 156
Leaving care, what's needed, 110
Leisure activities, 51-53
    I don't want to do anything, 53
    what to do in free time, 51
Lesbian, 74
Life story work, 25
    BAAF publication on, 25
Line manager for key worker, 9
Listening and being listened to, 92
Listening, simple rules, 92
Living accommodation, finding a place, 115
Living in a family, 95
Living with friends, 95
Locked up, when a young person's liberty may be restricted, 34
Lonely, what to do about it, 130
Loss and bereavement, 108
LSD, 64
Magic Mushrooms, 64
Management records, 160
Manager of team, of area, 9
Medicals, young person's right to refuse, 59
Meetings, minutes, 13
    planning, 15
    preparing agenda, 12
    purpose, 11
    timekeeping, 12
Mementos, value of, 24
Methadone, 64
Money, 37
    budgeting check list, 41
    learning to manage, 37
    managing, budgeting/saving, 39
    what a young person needs to think about, 39
Mood, sudden swings in, 63
Mosque, 31
Music, what can I do, 51
Name, can I change my name, 163
National Foster Care Association, 113, 164
Nationality and ethnicity, 140
Needles, getting clean, 65
Neglect, 103
Netball team, benefits of, 53
Noise, damage to health, 54
NVQ, national vocational qualifications for carers, 6
    qualifications for young people, 48

Parental responsibility, 162
    who has it, 162
Parents, what the Children Act 1989 says, 21
    working with, 21
    working with, importance of plan for contact, 21
Parr, Margaret, 29
Partnership with families, 21, 23
    with young people, 5
Periods, 56
Permissible forms of control, 85
Personal and sexual relationships, is it for real, 74
Personal Hygiene, 56
Personal relationships and sex, 71
Places to live, 32
Planning meetings, 15
    what happens afterwards, 16
    what should be on the plan, 15
    who can speak, 16
    who goes, 15
Poor attendance at school, 43
Postqualifying and advanced awards in social work, 6, 7
Pregnant, what to do, 73
Prejudice, 91
Prejudice, see discrimination
Privacy and confidentiality, 87
Problems, sorting it out, 79
Prohibited Steps Order, 145
Promises, importance of carers keeping them, 92
Protection, young person's right to, 103-109
Punishment, official guidelines, 85
Qualifications and training for carers, 6, 7
    for young people, 48-50
Race Relations Act 1976, 28
Racial origin, 29-30
Rape, what it is, 71
Records, how long they are kept, 161
    how to see them, 160
    what's on them, 159
    young person's right to see them, 160
Religious persuasion, 29-30
Reporting officer, 153
Representations, under the Children Act, 26
Residence Order, 146
    and changing names, 163
Responsibilities and rights, for young people and carers, 1

Responsibilities carers, 4-5
Reviews, 17
    how often do they happen, 17
    what are they, 17
    who will be there, 18
Right and wrong, knowing the difference, 83
Rights and responsibilities, carers, 1
    young people, 1
Running away, 103
Safe sex, 73
Sanctions, need for them to be fair, 83
School, effects of changing, 45
    starting a new one, 45
    staying on or going to college, 46
    subjects to study, 45
    what to do after, 46
Schooling, ideas, to help young people, 44
Secrets, those that cannot be kept, 87
Secure Units, 34
    when might I be sent to one, 34
    when can my liberty be restricted, 34
Sedatives, 64
Self-esteem, 88
Self-respect, building self-esteem, young people, 88
Sentences for breaking the law, 157
Sex and personal relationships, 71
Sex and the law, 71
Sex Discrimination Act 1975, 28
Sexism, 91
Sexual relationship, right to say no, 72
    what young people might think about, 72
    deciding not to, 72
Sleep, importance of in health, 54
Smack, 64
Smoking, 56
    passive, 56
Solvent abuse, 67
    how to help, 69
    how to minimize harm, 69
    substances involved, 65
    what to look for, 68
    why they do it, 67
Special needs, qualifications for young people with, 49
Specific Issue Order, 146
Speed, 64
Sport, what can I do, 51

Steroids, anabolic, 64
Suicide attempts, 103
for emotional distress generally see 92-102
Sulph, 64
Suntan, 59
Supervision Order, 147
Support for carers, 6-9
Talking about the past, 24
Talking tool: one of the aims of the handbook, 2
Telephone numbers and addresses, 164-169
Telling the truth, 91
The Children Act 1989, a young person's
    background, 29
        general aims, 2
        recognizing differences, 29
Training and qualifications for carers, 6, 7
Tranquillisers, 64
Values, 91
Vol, 64
Wardship and Inherent Jurisdiction, 155
Weed, 64
Weight, importance in health, 55
Whizz, 64
Work permit, 76
    getting one, 76
Work finding work, 117-118
    keeping a job, 127-128
    preparing for interviews, 124
    starting work, what I need to know, 128
    what can I do, 77
Working part time, 76
Working, applying for 117-120
Worries, 98
    checklist, 101
    physical symptoms, 96
    psychological symptoms, 96
Youth Justice, 156